COLLECTION MANAGEMENT IN THE ELECTRONIC AGE:

A MANUAL FOR CREATING COMMUNITY COLLEGE COLLECTION DEVELOPMENT POLICY STATEMENTS

CJCLS Guide #1

Edited by

Jennie S. Boyarski
Paducah Community College

Kate Hickey
Pennsylvania College of Technology

Community and Junior College Libraries Section
Association of College and Research Libraries
American Library Association

Published by the Association of College and Research Libraries
A Division of the American Library Association
50 East Huron Street
Chicago, IL 60611

ISBN 0-8389-7737-5

Printed on recycled paper.

Printed in the United States of America.

CONTENTS

This survey and publication are sponsored by the Ad Hoc Committee on Research and Publications, Community and Junior College Libraries Section, Association of College and Research Libraries, American Library Association.

Expressions of appreciation to:

Edna Driver, Library Secretary, Paducah Community College
Linda Morgan, Library Secretary, Pennsylvania College of Technology
Mailing and Duplicating Department of Pennsylvania College of Technology

INTRODUCTION

Collection development has been defined as the planned purchase of materials in all formats to match instructional and research needs of the campus within the current fiscal restraints and resource sharing opportunities.[1]

The definition should also include weeding or deselection responsibilities. The process should be evaluated in light of the following considerations:

1. Are management of the acquisition allocations and authority for establishing the selection process explicit?

2. Does the collection development policy reflect the instructional and research priorities of the college?

3. Are all forms of information access addressed? Cooperative collection development plans, remote access, networks, etc.

4. Is there an organized review of the collection outlined to ensure a viable collection?

5. Are collection formats technologically current?

6. Are procedures for managing challenged materials included?

7. Are gift policies and procedures provided?

Because current methods of information access require hi-tech equipment, the cost of materials is only a portion of the expense of doing business.

Since larger collections are limited by shrinking budgets and space constraints, more emphasis should be given to cooperative collection development and local, state, and national networks. The growth of the electronic and remote access of information should influence the appropriateness of locally owned materials. No longer is ownership necessarily equated to quality of information services. A balance between owning and accessing sources now is the key to effective collection management decisions.

[1] Breivik, Patricia and E. Gordon Gee. Information Literacy; Revolution in the Library. (Washington, DC: American Council on Education, 1989) 109.

Though the format of information changes, librarians' commitment to academic freedom is evidenced by the inclusion of the "Library Bill of Rights" and "Freedom to View" documents in collection development statements.

The following pages reflect an array of approaches for managing information access in community and junior colleges. All academic libraries must have written policies to effectively guide this major function and to ensure responsible fiscal management.

BACKGROUND AND SURVEY RESULTS

When in the summer of 1993 the editors distributed the "CJCLS Survey of Collection Development Policies" to just over 350 community and junior college libraries, little did we expect a response rate of 202 replies, with 69 libraries taking the time to send samples of their policies. More than ninety individual comments were added to the statistical responses. This overwhelming response indicates a nationwide interest in the fast-changing world of collection development.

HISTORY

This manual grew out of the formation of the CJCLS Ad Hoc Committee on Research and Publication at the midwinter ALA meeting in San Antonio January 1992. The founding members perceived a need to encourage and sponsor ALA publications relating directly to two-year academic institutions. Beverley Gass of Guilford Technical Community College, Jamestown NC, has served as the chair since the committee's inception.

After developing guidelines, consulting with similar ACRL committees, and surveying section members, the committee decided on an initial technical guide format, similar to ACRL CLIP Notes. In 1993, after several false starts, the committee chose the topic of audiovisual materials collection development and appointed Jennie Boyarski as editor. Later the scope was broadened to include collection development policies for all formats -- print, audiovisual, and electronic -- and Kate Hickey signed on as co-editor.

In July 1993 the "CJCLS Survey of Collection Development Policies" (see Appendix) was mailed to 357 members of the Community and Junior College Libraries Section. Care was taken to send to only one person per library. Immediately following the original August 15th deadline, the editors sent a postcard reminder to those who had not responded, offering a second copy of the survey and extending the response deadline to August 30. As mentioned above, by September 1, 202 librarians had responded with usable completed surveys.

SURVEY RESULTS

Survey respondents represent a broad range of library sizes. Approximately two-thirds of the libraries are in colleges with fewer than 5000 FTE's and have fewer than 15 full-time library staff. Most of these have book collections of 75,000 titles or less and subscribe to fewer than 500 periodical titles. Somewhat surprisingly 77% report less than 20 electronic titles, including CD-ROM products, computer programs for public use, and locally-mounted databases.

Answers to survey questions relating to acquisition budgets reveal the well-known fact that most libraries are operating under serious fiscal constraints. In spite of the growing quantity and cost of library resources, most libraries -- 80% or more -- have print budgets of $100,000 or less, periodicals budgets of $50,000 or less, audiovisual materials budgets of $25,000 or less, and electronics resources budgets of $30,000 or less. These limited dollars make it all the more imperative for librarians to spend wisely according to current, comprehensive collection development plans.

The editors are particularly interested in how libraries are countering acquisition constraints with alternatives to permanent ownership. Ninety-eight percent offer interlibrary loan services; 68% perform online searches for patrons; 63% videotape off-air and off-satellite; and 44% purchase site or blanket software licenses. One-third or less of the respondents participate in cooperative collection development with other libraries, access resources for patron through the Internet, or purchase documents on demand from commercial vendors.

Fees for such services are relatively rare. About 20% charge patrons for online searching, with community borrowers more likely to be charged than faculty or students. Interestingly, 15% of libraries charge for interlibrary loan in all cases. Otherwise, the above services incur no user fees in 94% of all surveyed libraries.

Over 80% of libraries responding have written collection development policies, and nearly that many have written de-selection or weeding policies as well. While many commented that their policies are out-dated, sixty-nine felt theirs were current enough to share. These documents form the bulk of this manual.

A full compilation of survey results is included in the Appendix.

OVERVIEW OF COLLECTION DEVELOPMENT POLICY STATEMENTS

A significant number of collection development policy statements were submitted with the Community and Junior College Library Section (CJCLS) Survey of Collection Development Policies. Those chosen for this publication are representative of the CJCLS Section's membership. The editors selected statements from large and small institutions as well as from districts. Some of the policies are very general while others are extremely specific. Some are written in a narrative style and others take an outline approach. Some of the partial documents represent uniqueness or a particularly strong statement.

EXEMPLARY POLICIES

Several college libraries' documents are printed in total. The collection begins with the clear, concise and general statements of St. Louis Community College. The document could be adopted in total with few revisions and contains most elements appropriate for a collection development policy. This is a particularly noteworthy document in this time of rapid change in information access. It avoids commitment to specifics and stresses the relationship between access and ownership.

Washtenaw Community College's comprehensive policies detail the guidelines for selection of library materials including special collections such as reserve materials and annual reports. The audiovisual materials selection criteria are definitively written. This is a living document which serves as a daily guide for library procedures and is detail specific to format. Such comprehensive policies are not limited to large or multi-type institutions such as Washtenaw. Warren County Community College's similarly complete policy statements serve a student population of less than one thousand.

Pierce College's statements are technologically current and approach collection development from both the format and subject point of view. On the other hand, the College of DuPage, a very large institution, offers a policy with a more theoretical and narrative direction. A large percentage of the document is devoted to a systematic appraisal of the current collection.

Specific responsibilities for the main library and its branches, as well as the sectors, are outlined in the Houston Community College System's document. The Austin Community College plan is more general. Criteria for material formats are outlined and collection maintenance is detailed; however, the reference is system wide. Cedar Valley's statements are detail specific with delegation to specific staff members. The format of the document is unique with the pages divided between responsibilities and actions.

An excellent example of a succinctly written collection development policy is that of the College of the Desert's Copper Mountain Campus. The introduction clearly states the principles and guidelines for the selection procedure. General acquisition guidelines are delineated with additional criteria for books and serials.

The subject specific approach is evident in several of the publications. Chippewa Valley Technical College uses the subject conspectus approach with self-defined definitions. A chart reporting format records the levels of program support and the weeding policies by LC schedule. Marian Court Junior College, on the other hand, uses the standard conspectus definitions and analyzes them by the Dewey schedule. McIntosh College establishes an in-depth narrative collection development statement arranged by college program. The statements include references to on-line access where appropriate. Several examples of the McIntosh policies are included in this manual.

NOTEWORTHY SPECIFICS

Most of the documents contain weeding, gift, and challenged materials policies. Washtenaw's gift statement which references periodicals is particularly noteworthy. Both Guilford Technical Community College and Lower Columbia College offer model donor information and consent forms. Neither library appraises materials. Guilford offers the donor the opportunity to reclaim titles that are not acceptable for inclusion in the library collection. Warren County's reconsideration and challenged materials guidelines are excellent. The procedures and the request for review forms are worthy of adoption.

Although most of the documents contain weeding or deselection statements, those from Hillsborough Community College District and Glendale Community College represent different approaches to the process. Hillsborough systematically reviews materials by general subjects and formats (i.e. technology, social science, fiction, encyclopedias, almanacs). Glendale sets specific guidelines by the Dewey Decimal Classification System. Both views have merit. Obviously the district guidelines are more general.

In addition to the expected policy topics, Austin Community College offers criteria for remotely stored materials which are referenced in public access catalogs and are only available through the college's delivery system.

Although the Americans with Disabilities Act is a popular topic for articles and conferences, most of the policies mention only services for the visually impaired. However, St. Petersburg Community College's treatment of special needs is comprehensive and includes a list of sources for bibliographies on disabilities.

ELECTRONIC ACCESS

Electronic formats and services, current hot topics in librarianship, are seldom mentioned. On the traditional side, the College of DuPage addresses the selection of locally produced media software. Several colleges outline media equipment criteria. St. Louis District guidelines define instructional resource equipment and establish the criteria for equipment selection.

Lansing Community College makes the following statement about database services:

> A database service (on-line and/or CD-ROM) will be considered on the basis of the subject material, its accessibility and completeness. Information provided by the database should address LCC client needs. Criteria such as user-friendliness and easy access to the information, as well as hardware requirements and interfaceability with other services will be used in the selection process. Consideration will also be given to the completeness of the material in terms of citation, abstract, and/or full-text formats. [2]

CD-ROM is mentioned by several as an option for indices, periodicals, print materials, and audio-visuals. The only mention of CD-ROM and computer software as a separate format is Marion Court Junior College's collection description:

> "[CD-Rom and computer software] collecting decisions should take into consideration the expected longevity of the format, hardware needs, long-term costs (such as licensing requirements and maintaining currency), amount and type of user instruction needed, as well as whether the particular format offers any distinct advantages over other formats in which the material is available."[3]

Networking and cooperative collection development are addressed primarily by multi-library districts. The St. Louis plan does expand the definition of networking beyond the district; however, the reference focuses on interlibrary loan activities only. Cooperative collection development is not evident at this time.

[2] Lansing Community College. Library Information Services. Collection Development Policy. Revised 1991. p.5.

[3] Marion Court Junior College. Lindsay Library. Collection Development Policy. no date, no page number.

No matter the format, the number of titles and who is responsible for the selection of information in community college libraries, the college and the library's mission statements should guide the process. Tarrant County Junior College District's mission and goals statements are noteworthy because they clearly provide the appropriate direction for those responsible for collection development activities.

FACTORS INFLUENCING COLLECTION DEVELOPMENT TODAY

Although none of the statements mention the relationship between local collections and remote information access, the availability of databases via the INTERNET and the concept of the virtual library are changing the complexion of locally owned collections. Access versus ownership is the issue challenging library managers. The future of the National Information Infrastructure, the possible privatization of the INTERNET and the expansion of cooperative collection development activities will be major factors in library collection development decisions.

Collection development control is shifting from classroom faculty to librarians to ensure a balanced comprehensive collection. The information explosion, shrinking budgets and the increased number of formats require selectors with a broad understanding of the complex issues involved.

Off-campus programs and non-traditional methods of instruction effect the scope of local library collections. Dial access and virtual instruction pave the way for more information on demand and less acquisition of materials in the hope of need.

Balancing this finely tuned process will more than challenge library personnel. Academic libraries in transition are facing changes in mission, scope and information format. The following documents can provide guidance to librarians attempting to meet the daily challenge of bringing materials and users together.

MODEL POLICY STATEMENTS

Complete Documents

Collection Development Statement

St. Louis Community College
Instructional Resources
Revised January, 1990

St. Louis
Community College

TABLE OF CONTENTS

I. INTRODUCTION

St. Louis Community College is a public two-year institution located in the central eastern portion of Missouri. The College offers its educational services at three campuses, two educational centers, and numerous extension centers. The service area consists of St. Louis city, St. Louis county, and portions of Franklin and Jefferson counties.

The College offers a broad array of academic and training opportunities. It awards associate in arts (AA), associate in applied science (AAS), and associate in science (AS) degrees, certificates of proficiency, and certificates of specialization, and it provides many additional educational opportunities.

The college transfer programs lead to the AA degree. While the catalogs detail eleven different transfer curricula, all provide the first two years of a baccalaureate program. Over 100 career programs lead to certificates of specialization, certificates of proficiency, and AAS degrees. The College also offers a number of developmental courses for students who are underprepared for college work, most of them in basic skills--mathematics, reading, and writing.

Continuing Education offers a vast variety of credit and non-credit offerings at more than 50 diverse community locations. It also offers specialized 'customized' training and re-training programs for local business and industry.

Within St. Louis Community College, Instructional Resources has been assigned the responsibility for the development of library and media services which support the instructional goals of the College. Each campus has an Instructional Resources division with a technical services department located at the College Center.

Instructional Resources has collection development as one of its most important tasks. Collection development includes the selection of appropriate instructional material and equipment and, also, the continued re-evaluation and maintenance of these items.

The purpose of this statement is to develop a college-wide document which will define the collection development program and will provide necessary guidance for building and maintaining the material and equipment collections.

II. PHILOSOPHY AND MISSION OF THE COLLEGE

St. Louis Community College recognizes the dignity and worth of all human beings and believes that postsecondary education should be available to all who can benefit from it. The College further believes that education should be a rewarding experience offered in an environment that fosters the growth and well-being of all members of the community it serves.

The mission of St. Louis Community College is to provide to its constituents and community comprehensive post-secondary programs and services that are academically, geographically, and financially accessible. To this end, the College assumes responsibility and leadership in responding to the multiple educational and training needs of its diverse community and is committed to delivery of high quality instruction and support programs to the broad range of students who are qualified and who can benefit from formal instruction. The College will seek to achieve this mission within the limits of its legal and fiscal capabilities.
(Foreword to Board Policy)

III. OBJECTIVES OF THE INSTRUCTIONAL RESOURCES PROGRAM

The following statements reflect the objectives of the instructional resources program:

1. To provide leadership and assistance in the development of instructional systems and materials which employ effective and efficient means of accomplishing those institutional and instructional objectives.

2. To provide an organized and readily accessible collection of materials and supportive equipment needed to meet institutional, instructional, and individual needs of students, staff, and faculty.

3. To provide a staff qualified, concerned, and involved in serving the needs of the students, faculty, staff, and community.

4. To encourage innovation, learning, and community services by providing facilities and resources which will make them possible.

IV. OBJECTIVES OF THE COLLECTION DEVELOPMENT PROGRAM

The collection development program is an on-going activity which is designed to meet the following objectives:

1. To provide materials and equipment to support and meet the instructional, institutional, and individual needs of students, faculty, and staff.

2. To provide a mechanism for instructional faculty participation in the development of the collection.

3. To provide an integrated collection of print and non-print materials.

4. To provide quantitative and philosophical diversity/balance in relation to curricula, programs, course, and personal development needs of the students, faculty, and staff.

5. To respond to the heterogeneity of the student body.

6. To provide centralized collections when appropriate.

7. To provide a college-wide basis for evaluation of the collection as well as each campus location.

8. To respond to the local and regional resources available to students, faculty, and staff.

9. To provide the basis for budget planning and use for the current and future years.

V. RESPONSIBILITY FOR COLLECTION DEVELOPMENT

Ultimate responsibility at each location rests with the Associate Dean for Instructional Resources at each campus and the Director of Instructional Resources Technical Services at the Community College Center. Instructional Resources directors are usually delegated the operational responsibility of the collection development program.

Instructional Resources faculty and staff are assigned selection responsibilities for library and media collections. In addition, instructional faculty make recommendations for print and non-print material to support the curricula. Instructional Resources faculty are assigned responsibility for the development of one or more subject areas of the collection. To insure that the materials they select support the curricula, the Instructional Resources faculty and staff consult with instructional faculty in the divisions/departments representing their assigned subject areas and they may also attend those divisions' and departments' meetings as needed.

Instructional Resources faculty and staff encourage the participation of all segments of the College community in the collection development program--inviting requests for new materials, routing review materials, involving them in previewing and evaluating non-print material, and consulting them during collection reevaluation.

VI. DESCRIPTION OF THE CLIENTELE SERVED

Instructional Resources' clientele is composed of the student body, the College's faculty and staff, and residents of the community.

Because St. Louis Community College offers an open-door admissions policy as well as a wide variety of educational programs, its student body is a diverse group of individuals. The students are as diverse in their personal goals as they are in their educational goals. There are full-time students attending college parallel courses during the day session, students with full-time jobs attending evening classes on a part-time basis, students enrolled in technical and vocational programs, as well as those enrolled in non-credit, continuing education courses.

Although the student body is heterogeneous, certain characteristics and trends of the student body as a whole can be identified. Many of the students are in transition; they have made the decision to attend school in response to circumstances in their lives such as a job change, new interests, a divorce, or retirement. Not only are the individuals in transition, but the student body as well. The average age of students has been increasing steadily over the years. There are more part-time students than full-time students and more women than men attending the College. Greater numbers of students are attending classes at off-site locations and the numbers of physically-handicapped and educationally-disabled students have increased.

VII. PHILOSOPHY OF SERVICES

The services and the collection of Instructional Resources are available to all members of the College community: students, faculty, staff, and the community.

In the use of Instructional Resources materials, the Instructional Resources faculty work with the students and serve as adjunct teachers for all departments, acting as interpreters and intermediaries between professor and students. The Instructional Resources faculty member has a unique opportunity to help students expand their intellectual horizons, see relationships between various areas of their studies, appreciate resource materials as a means of intellectual stimulus and growth, clarify student assignments, learn expert use of the library's resources, and become aware of the utility of individual reference works. Instructional Resources encourages students enrolled in off-campus programs to make use of the on-campus facilities and, in addition, provides materials directly to off-campus sites.

Service is also available to faculty and staff. For these groups, searches are made which support the process of instruction, the smooth flow of administration, and the overall objectives of the College. Personal information needs of faculty and staff of necessity are given secondary attention. Instructional Resources staff stay abreast of the resources in the area; thus the research needs of faculty, staff, and students beyond the capabilities of the campus Instructional Resources may be appropriately referred to special collections in area libraries.

Community residents as taxpayers are served as their needs require and as reference staff time allows. A significant part of service to community residents is instruction in the purposes and proximity of libraries more primary to their needs.

VIII. INTELLECTUAL FREEDOM

Implementation of the concept of academic freedom in Instructional Resources involves selecting some materials which may be considered controversial by some individuals or groups. Reasons often cited for materials considered offensive may include profanity, divergent viewpoints, controversial authors, sexual explicitness, use of non-

standard English and dialects, and violence and criminal acts. The acquisition of such material does not imply approval or endorsement of contents. These materials are acquired to support the curriculum and to represent all sides of controversial issues. The selection criteria used by St. Louis Community College must remain broad and flexible in order to provide a collection which supports the broad range of academic programs and diverse backgrounds of its clientele.

Procedures for handling complaints include allowing citizen(s) to complete a form requesting that the material be reconsidered and appropriate administrative review. The form is available at each Instructional Resources location of the College.

To compliment the statement in Board Policy on academic freedom, Instructional Resources also affirms the principles contained in the "Library Bill of Rights" and "Freedom to View."[1] Copies of both documents are available at each Instructional Resources location.

IX. COPYRIGHT

It is the policy of St. Louis Community College to support the property and copyrights of the creators and their assigns to the materials contained in the collections of St. Louis Community College as encompassed in the Copyright Act of 1976 as Amended.

The College further recognizes the need for the *fair use* of those materials in the pursuit of the mission of the College.

X. STANDARDS

Two sets of guidelines have been developed which provide a means of comparing individual facilities, staffs, and materials with recommended minimum and maximum levels of adequacy. Instructional Resources supports both sources in regard to the statements on collection development. "Guidelines for Two-Year College Learning Resources Programs" provides guidance in the selection of equipment in Section III, H-J and materials in section D, 1-14.[2] This document has been approved by the American Library Association, the American Association of Community and Junior Colleges, and the Association for Educational Communication and Technology. The second source, "Statement on Quantitative Standards for Two-Year Learning Resources Programs," has been approved by the Association of College and Research Libraries, which is a division of the American Library Association.[3]

College activities which use the guidelines cited above include the curriculum proposals submitted to the Coordinating Board of Higher Education and self-studies written for accrediting associations. The Coordinating Board's "Program Review Policies and Procedures" specifically requests that the library be evaluated according to the "standards of the Association of College and Research Libraries or any other recognized measure..."[4] Accreditation self-studies often ask for a general measure of the collection along with specific questions related to materials for the program being evaluated.

The guidelines are used internally for planning and evaluation.

XI. DEFINITION OF MATERIALS

Materials which are under the jurisdiction of Instructional Resources are those print and non-print materials which are specifically designed to support the instructional objectives of the College and the instructional resources program. These materials include books, periodicals and other serials, government documents, pamphlets, technical and research reports, microforms, sound recordings, films/video recordings, pictures, slides, photographs, kits, realia, and computer software regardless of whether they are obtained by purchase, lease, rental, loan, gift, exchange or local production.

1."Library Bill of Rights," adopted by the American Library Association, June 18, 1948. Amended February 2, 1961, June 27, 1967, and January 23, 1980 by the ALA Council. "Freedom to View," adopted by the Board of Directors of the Association for Educational Communications and Technology, December 1, 1979, and the ALA Council in June, 1979.

2."Guidelines for Two-Year College Learning Resources Programs," approved by the Association of College and Research Libraries Board of Directors, June 30, 1981. (Copies of this document are available at each Instructional Resources location.)

3."Statement on Quantitative Standards for Two-Year Learning Resources Programs," approved by the Association of College and Research Libraries Board of Directors, June, 1979. (Copies of this document are available at each Instructional Resources location.)

4."Program Review Policies and Procedures," adopted by the Coordinating Board for Higher Education, Missouri Department of Higher Education, September, 1978, p. 15.

Materials which are not under the jurisdiction of Instructional Resources include textbooks, laboratory manuals, desk copies, and consumable instructional supplies which are all independent of the Instructional Resources program.

XII. CRITERIA FOR SELECTION OF MATERIALS

The Instructional Resources staff selects print and non-print materials from professional selection tools, professional journals, standard bibliographies and, in some cases, from publisher's catalogs.

The following criteria are used to evaluate materials considered for addition to the collection:

1. Appropriateness of the medium.
2. Correlation to the existing collection.
3. Literary style and quality.
4. Author's expertise.
5. Technical quality.
6. Organization.
7. Timeliness/permanence.
8. Insight into the human condition.
9. Scarcity of material available on the subject.
10. Demand.
11. Price/relative cost of material in relation to the budget and other available materials.
12. Appropriateness of material for the clientele.
13. Relevance to instructional needs.

Re-Evaluation is the regular and continuous process of selecting material that is worn, out of date, inaccurate or no longer circulating, for withdrawal from Instructional Resources holdings.

Materials in the collection are subject to the same evaluation criteria applied to acquisitions. Circulating and reference works which have been superceded or are found to contain inaccurate (e.g., errors of fact in technical subject areas) or poorly presented information, or otherwise fail to fulfill the collection's purposes will be removed from the collection. Teaching departments are consulted for this process. All withdrawals are subject to approval of the Director of Library Services and/or Media Services. Withdrawn titles are disposed of in accordance with College procedures.

Titles withdrawn because of loss, damage, or general condition are considered for replacement. Classics are replaced whenever possible in improved format or edition.

The same considerations applied in original selection apply to replacements, in addition, other factors must be considered:

1. Availability of newer and better materials in the field.

2. The value of the individual title, whether for literary quality, subject appeal, or authority and importance of the author.

3. Requests for the title or subject.

XIII. DEFINITION OF EQUIPMENT

Instructional Resources equipment is any non-consumable device that facilitates the use of instructional materials and programming which require equipment to make them visible and/or audible. Included in this equipment group are projectors, audio and visual playback machines, telecommunications equipment, data processing equipment, and associated mass storage devices.

Instructional Resources equipment also includes that equipment necessary to locally produce materials in support of the instructional goals of the College. Included in this group are video and audio recorders, cameras, and all other peripheral support equipment.

XIV. EQUIPMENT SELECTION CRITERIA

Instructional Resources selects that equipment which supports its goals and objectives. The following criteria are used to evaluate equipment:

1. The equipment must have campus-wide use or potential for campus-wide use.

2. The equipment must perform to accepted standards. If an industry or educational standard format is available, Instructional

Resources shall endeavor to select equipment that conforms to that format. If no standard format exists, the Instructional Resources staff will attempt to select that equipment which appears to have the best chance for success in the marketplace.

3. The equipment must be able to play materials from more than one vendor.

4. The equipment for use by patrons shall be easy to operate with a minimum of training.

5. The equipment must be designed to withstand use by many different operators and withstand normal instructional use.

6. The cost and ease of maintenance shall be considered in selection.

7. The relevance to instructional needs shall be considered in selection.

8. Instructional Resources will make recommendations with regard to existing campus inventory of equipment to insure compatibility and lower cost of parts and supply stocks.

Instructional Resources specifies all media equipment using the above criteria and offers assistance to departments with specialized needs. Purchases made through grants should be routed through Instructional Resources for specifications and to insure compatibility with existing campus equipment. Instructional Resources will provide maintenance on all equipment purchased through Instructional Resources and on that equipment purchased with restricted funds per Instructional Resources developed specifications.

XV. BUDGET

Instructional Resources at each location is responsible for developing and defending a proposed budget according to the college-wide principles set forth each year. Customarily, the basis for this proposal is the previous budget with estimated adjustments upward to counteract the rate of inflation. These increases are based on projected percentages by Missouri's Coordinating Board for Higher Education. In addition, any extraordinary support which may be needed for new courses and new curricula or a marked shift in student population needs must be taken into account. Participation in curriculum committees, Instructional Resources staff contact with classroom and laboratory faculty, and needs of students documented through reference interviews aid in the determination of areas requiring special attention.

Instructional Resources does not allocate specific amounts of its materials budget to the individual subject areas of the collection. This allows for the accommodation of unanticipated changes in the curricula and in patron demand. The needs of the various subject areas in the collection vary considerably; flexibility allows, ultimately, for better services in all areas.

Only in exceptional circumstances do other divisions/departments provide for instructional materials.

XVI. NETWORKING

Interlibrary loan can be defined as the process in which library materials of one library are made available to another library for use by their patrons. On the College level, the three campus libraries make their materials available to each other through inter-campus loan. Those materials unavailable within the College are obtained for students, faculty, and staff by the College's Instructional Resources Technical Services Department from the appropriate lending institution. Materials requested on interlibrary loan are limited to those materials the library does not own and which cannot be obtained at a moderate cost. All interlibrary loan requests are made in consideration of the copyright law, the American Library Association's interlibrary loan code, and the policies of the lending institution, network, or cooperative system. The College's memberships in the Higher Education Center and the St. Louis Regional Library Network enable students, faculty, and staff to utilize the collections of other participating institutions. Direct borrowing privileges are available for full-time faculty, administrators and professional librarians through the Learning Resources Council's Reciprocal Borrowing Program and for faculty, staff and students through the St. Louis Regional Library Network's InfoPass Program.

The reference librarians at each location determine the appropriate method for securing materials from other libraries and make the necessary arrangements for doing so.

XVII. GIFTS & DONATIONS

Instructional Resources will accept gifts provided that the following conditions are met:

1. All gifts must be accepted in accordance with Board Policy 2.9.
2. Gifts of materials and/or equipment are evaluated for appropriateness to the College's collection using the same criteria applied to other acquisitions.
3. Instructional Resources will not provide donors with monetary evaluations of gifts.

XVIII. PROVISION FOR REVIEW

This document will be reviewed as needed by the Library Services Committee and the Media Services Committee. It will be approved by the District Instructional Resources Committee and forwarded to the District Curriculum Committee and District Academic Affairs Council.

The Learning Resource Center

Washtenaw Community College

Collection Development Statement

January 1986
Revised December 1988, October 1989

CONTENTS

APPENDICES

I. PURPOSE OF THE COLLECTION DEVELOPMENT STATEMENT

The purpose of the Collection Development Statement is to provide the basis for the systematic development of the Washtenaw Community College Learning Resource Center (LRC) library collections. The statement sets forth the criteria to be met in selecting books, serials, audiovisuals, computer programs, and other forms of research materials.

This codification of policies will serve to inform the LRC staff of the aims of the Collection Development Program and to help them understand and interpret the programs. It will enable the faculty to conceptualize LRC objectives and to cooperate in developing strong and balanced collections. It will provide the college administration with a definitive plan of current LRC acquisitions policies so that the role of the LRC can be clearly determined in the master planning for the campus.

Learning resource centers are growing and evolving institutions. Therefore, the librarians and other LRC professionals must be responsive to change and seek to keep the statement current with College educational policies, changes in the formats and delivery of information, and characteristics of our College populations. Regular review of the Collection Development Statement will occur and will involve College staff as appropriate.

II. OBJECTIVES OF THE LEARNING RESOURCE CENTER

A. To provide an organized and readily accessible collection of print and non-print materials and supportive equipment to meet institutional, instructional and individual needs of students and staff.

   1. The LRC Collection should support the College curriculum with:

      a) Adequate research materials for student use
      b) Supplementary reading selections
      c) A diversified reference collection
      d) A range of periodicals
      e) Non-print materials including traditional and newly developed audiovisual and computer (machine readable) formats.

B. To support institutional research of faculty or staff which relates to present or future curricular issues in higher education, and specifically community colleges.

C. To provide services which support the above objectives.

D. To encourage innovation and learning by providing facilities and resources which will make these possible.

E. To instruct users in the most expeditious means of research.

F. To assist faculty in development of instructional media and/or instructional systems.

III. CLIENTELE OF THE LRC

The students registered for courses or programs on this campus and at extension centers as well as the faculty, administrators and the support staff of the institution are the clientele of the WCC Learning Resource Center for whom the collections are developed.

Understanding the needs of these LRC users is the basic premise in the philosophy of collection development. Each title selected should fill a current or foreseeable need for some faction of the LRC's clientele.

Service will be extended beyond this defined group, but materials will not be specifically acquired for individuals and groups where need does not overlap with the above defined clientele.

IV. RESPONSIBILITY FOR THE SELECTION OF LRC MATERIALS

A. Librarians' Role in the Materials Selection Program

The librarians have the responsibility for the overall development of the LRC collections. Intrinsic in this charge are the following functions:

1) Making judgments as to the completeness of the holdings;

2) Considering every order in light of the needs of the LRC as a whole;

3) Determining the relative importance of monographs, serials, periodicals, and audiovisuals;

4) Selecting, with or without faculty consultation, such materials as the writings of specific authors, studies of the contemporary culture and other student interests that the librarians become aware of through their public service and reference contacts.

   Within the framework of the Collection Development Program the librarians will be assigned to certain subject areas to work in conjunction with faculty in the selection of current and retrospective materials. The librarians will review the selection of titles requested by faculty members and may question the appropriateness of orders. Librarians will select materials for their assigned subject areas, concentrating on retrospective and current titles. It is essential that the librarians establish and maintain a climate of cooperation with faculty members.

B. Faculty Participation in the Collection Development Program

Determination of the educational resources of the WCC Learning Resource Center is a professional consideration of great magnitude, requiring the cooperative efforts of librarians and faculty members with the LRC director.

Any WCC faculty member may recommend the purchase of books, serials, and media software in his subject area or curriculum to an LRC librarian. For book recommendations, the recommended titles will be reviewed by the librarian selector in that subject area and sent to the order department (Technical Services) if considered an appropriate addition. If the title cost is excessive as determined by an annual book average figure, the LRC director is consulted before ordering.

All serials requests are reviewed by the committee of the LRC director and librarians. Few new serials titles are ordered annually without corresponding elimination of other current subscriptions. (Exceptions are made for curricular support in new program areas.)

Audiovisual and computer format requests are regularly reviewed by the media librarian and by the Committee of LRC director and librarians at least once during the fall and winter semesters.

See Also:
- Media Selection and Acquisition Guidelines (Appendix I).
- Guidelines for Selection of Periodicals (Appendix II).

The librarians encourage the active participation of faculty members in the selection process. They encourage regular consultation regarding library support of course assignments and changed or new curricula.

C. Students' Role in the Materials Selection Process

Students, as prime users of the LRC, should be encouraged to contribute to the development of the collection by suggesting new titles and by assessing weaknesses in the holdings.

D. Final Responsibility in the Materials Selection Program

The responsibility for the development of the LRC collection rests ultimately with the LRC director.

The selection process is carried out by the librarians with the participation of the faculty. Full professional judgment is exercised in the choice of titles and subjects for acquisition, in accordance with the LRC Collection Development Statement. Advice may be sought from the LRC Advisory Committee regarding acquisitions or gifts to the collection which represent policy developments or changes. The Committee will not be consulted over individual title decisions, however.

V. CRITERIA FOR CONSIDERATION OF LIBRARY BOOKS

The following criteria are observed by librarians in the selection of books for the collection:

1) High standards of quality in content, format, and/or literary merit;

2) Appropriateness for undergraduate use in general education and/or occupational programs;

3) Possibility of use for one or more courses;

4) A lacuna in a particular subject area;

5) Student interest if subject matter is of general or contemporary nature;

6) Author's reputation in the subject field;

7) Positive review evaluations in one or more of the accepted reviewing media and/or citations for the book in specialized bibliographies or indexes;

8) Permanence or timeliness of the book;

9) Assessment of the translator if book is a foreign language work;

10) Reputation of the publisher;

11) Only available treatment of a new or obscure subject.

VI. CRITERIA FOR CONSIDERATION OF MEDIA SOFTWARE

The selection of media software is generally more attuned to instructional methods than is book selection. Attention is devoted to the patron as a learner, to the subject content, and to the learning process.

The LRC recognizes the effectiveness of audiovisuals in the instructional process and wishes to provide a variety of media for LRC patrons. Audio visuals, or media software, include the following formats and comprise the non-print library collection: audio tapes, computer programs, films, filmstrips, film loops, games, kits, pictures, recordings, slides, video tapes, video discs.

An effort is made to preview all media software before considering for purchase. The requesting instructor and the media librarian observe the following criteria in the selection of media software:

1) High standards of quality in content and format;

2) Adequacy in mode of communication for the purpose intended;

3) Appropriateness of format and content to the learning experience intended;

4) Adequacy of physical characteristics for durability and frequent use;

5) Balance in subject content and user needs in the total LRC collection, print and non-print.

VII. GUIDING PRINCIPLES FOR THE SELECTION OF LIBRARY MATERIALS

A. Approval Plans

There is considerable evidence in library literature and LRC experience has confirmed that approval plans do not bring the most appropriate materials into the library. Therefore, the LRC will follow the more traditional methods of book selection involving faculty-library cooperation on a title-by-title basis. Exception to this policy is made occasionally when acquiring media software if a preview copy of the item or evaluative reviews are not available.

B. Commercially Sponsored Materials

Commercially or privately sponsored books, pamphlets and audiovisual materials will be acceptable for the LRC if they fulfill the following obligations:

1) The materials will supplement or enrich the curriculum;

2) The materials can meet the same high standards for selection as applied to original purchases;

3) The amount of institutional advertising will be kept to a minimum.

See Also:
-Free Materials
-Controversial Issues

C. Controversial Issues

Because the Learning Resource Center encourages the free exploration of ideas in the pursuit of knowledge and truth, the LRC will make available study materials that represent a broad range of thought. It shall be the right and the obligation of the librarian to select such materials.

Items selected should, whenever possible, represent equally all views of a controversial issue or should present a point of view balanced by other materials in the collection. To determine these qualities in a book, the librarians will make extensive evaluations utilizing a complete range of professional resources.

Censorship of materials held in the LRC, or under consideration for inclusion there, will be challenged by the librarians. It is recognized that censorship attempts are made by both individuals and organizations which seek to control the dissemination of public information.

There can be no attempt to censor controversial materials by placing them under special controls. (Limited numbers of books highly subject to mutilation or theft because of illustrations or subject content will be located in the circulation area. They will be accessible through the card catalog, however, and available for loan.) All sides of a disputed issue should be represented in the book collection and the pamphlet file to provide students with free access to representative thought so that they may formulate their own opinions.

If controversial books are destroyed, mutilated or for any reason removed from the LRC, they should be considered for replacement according to the same criteria used for any library materials; that is, if, in the opinion of the librarians and the faculty selector, the contents of the book are still considered important, then a replacement will be ordered.

This policy is in accordance with the Freedom to Read statement of the American Library Association.

See Also:
-Restriction of Materials

D. Copyright Compliance

The Learning Resource Center complies with the United States Copyright Law, P.L. 94-553, in both intent and practice. Materials acquired by acquisition or donation must acknowledge the rights of copyright owner -- the exclusive rights of reproduction, adaptation, publication, performance, and display -- as stated generally in Section 106.

LRC services, such as, audiovisual recording and production; reserve materials procedures, and microcomputer lab assistance must comply with copyright principles as do acquisition procedures.

All licenses or permissions granted by copyright owners to the LRC will be kept on file until materials are withdrawn from the collection.

See Also:
-Reserve Collection

E. Desiderata List

A desiderata list which includes desirable materials sought for the LRC but currently out-of-print; books considered too costly for current budgets; and notable works that could be suggested for gifts will be maintained by Technical Services.

Requests for out-of-print books will be sent to various used book dealers for searching and/or price quotation.

See Also:
-Rare Books

F. Documents of the Federal Government

Documents represent compilations of information prepared by agencies of the federal government.

The Learning Resource Center is not a government depository library. All publications of the Government Printing Office needed for the collections must be individually selected according to the potential usefulness of the document and the general criteria for LRC materials.

Systematic ordering by the librarians from Vertical File Index and recommended lists appearing in the professional journals will enable the library to acquire the most significant government publications. Scanning of the Monthly Catalog of Government Publications is also advised for a more complete coverage of this publishing source.

Government documents, as acquired will be cataloged for the collections or placed in the vertical file. They will be evaluated periodically and eliminated if they have become obsolete.

See Also:
-Regional Materials

G. Evaluation of the Collection

To maintain a collection of optimum usefulness, the librarians will engage in a continual evaluation of the books and periodicals held in the LRC collection. This process requires the same attention to quality and authoritativeness as the original selection of materials. The librarians will study portions of the book collection, examining the holdings for their currency, validity, and usefulness in the research process, comparing their assessments against the standard subject bibliographies for academic libraries and especially junior college libraries. The concurrence of faculty representatives in the subject disciplines evaluated will be sought, as necessary, before withdrawing any questionable materials.

Under no circumstances will materials be removed from the shelves because of partisan or doctrinal disapproval.

The concern of the librarians in evaluating and, in some instances, removing materials will be:

1) Books containing obsolete or inaccurate data or facts;

2) Superseded editions of books currently held by the LRC;

3) Incomplete sets of books, the continuity of which is not maintained;

4) Incomplete holdings of journals for which there is no adequate indexing service;

5) Multiple copies of titles for which there is not adequate justification;

6) Worn or badly marked or mutilated volumes.

See Also:
-Faculty Participation in Materials Selection Program

H. Faculty Research Materials

The LRC will acquire faculty research materials for the study and teaching of a subject but will carefully review faculty requests that are deemed highly specialized, excessively expensive, or inappropriate for research or teaching of a community college curriculum. In lieu of acquiring these definitive materials, the LRC will make every effort to locate and borrow the needed books and serials through interloan services available to the LRC.

Faculty and administrative staff doing research for institutional or instructional development or improvements may recommend the purchase of books for the LRC. The LRC will acquire materials if their addition to the collection will be of more than temporary value, i.e. will be of potential value for longer than the life of the project. These research materials will be evaluated by the same criteria as other titles requested. Attempts to meet the researcher's need with borrowed books or serials will be advised if requested titles are excessively expensive or of an ephemeral nature.

I. Foreign Language Materials

The majority of the books in the LRC will be written in the English language. Limited acquisition will occur, however, of literary titles in foreign languages which are taught in a two semester sequence at the College and for identified groups of foreign language students. The LRC will subscribe to at least one foreign language periodical per language course taught at the College.

J. Free Materials

The acquisition of free materials should be considered with some degree of realism and restraint. Only if the pamphlets, reports or books can be expected to fulfill a research need should they be acquired; otherwise, they create problems of processing, control and space consumption.

Furthermore, considerable caution should be taken to determine that any free materials sent to the library or ordered by the library do not contain strongly biased statements, distorting or misleading statements, or extensive commercial messages. In cases where strong views are presented, an attempt will be made to provide materials on all viewpoints.

See Also:
- -Pamphlets
- -Commercially Sponsored Materials

K. Gifts of Books and Periodicals

In general, the LRC is interested in receiving donations of books and other publications that will enrich the collection. Space requirements, however, necessitate keeping older issues of periodicals in microform. Therefore, seldom will gifts of periodical issues in paper format be accepted. Gifts of money designated for the purchase of certain book or other materials will also be accepted provided that the materials will be appropriate for use in the LRC.

Specifically, the LRC will follow these criteria for gift books:

1) Books and other publications received in the LRC as gifts will be reviewed for the same standards of excellence as applied to new materials being selected.

2) Gift materials must be of such nature that they can be integrated into the collection, not held separately thus requiring special facilities, controls and staffing.

3) Care should be given to the matter of keeping gift materials up-to-date. If the donations will require continuing obligations beyond reasonable limits, the donated materials, after thoughtful deliberation, should be rejected.

4) When contacted by a potential donor the LRC may request that a listing of the gift books and periodicals be provided in advance of the materials being brought to the LRC. The librarians will then assess the proffered materials and notify the donor as to those titles which are considered appropriate for the collection. The LRC also has the option of disposing of gift materials that are later found to be unusable, with those of value being forwarded to other libraries or put on a free rack for WCC students.

5) The LRC will abide by the regulations on gifts as stated in the Statement on Appraisal of Gifts of the Association of College and Research libraries Committee on Manuscripts Collection (1973).

See Also:
-Guidelines for the Accedptance of Gifts (Appendix III).

L. Materials for Visually Handicapped Students

The LRC will attempt to provide adequately for visually handicapped students. Because it would be impossible to acquire a vast cross disciplinary collection of large-print books or books on tape or in braille format, the librarians will attempt to work with individual students who have need for these specialized materials.

Utilizing the services of the Washtenaw County Library, which is a regional library of the Library of Congress, the librarians can borrow textbooks and parallel materials recommended by the instructor prepared in braille or in recorded form. Large-print books, mainly recreational reading, are also available from this source. The special services of the Washtenaw County Library are coordinated with the Library of Michigan, Library for the Blind, and with other leading agencies serving the visually and physically handicapped.

M. Materials Selection Aids

Because the output of book publishers has become so great and, further, because there should be total accountability for funds designated for the purchase of books by the LRC, the librarians must set and maintain high standards for the selection of materials. To augment their professional training in book selection, the librarians will consult the following resources in the process of evaluating new titles:

1) Book catalogs of other college libraries where there is an emphasis on undergraduate and/or two year programs;

2) Accession lists from esteemed libraries;

3) Standard scholarly bibliographies that parallel the curricular interests of WCC;

4) Studies of the literature of a given discipline;

5) Citation lists of important new books for academic libraries;

6) Review media such as Booklist, Library Journal, Times (London) Literary Supplement, Technical Book Review Index, New York Times Book Review, New York Review of Books and the book reviews prepared for the scholarly, literary and trade journals;

7) Booksellers' catalogs and advertising materials.

The following resources are consulted in the process of evaluating audiovisual and computer programs:

1) Review media listed in number six above, especially Booklist. Also, Landers Film Reviews, Software Reviews on File;

2) Trade journals and subject specific journals such as Byte and Creative Computing;

3) Regularly published reports such as Library Technology Reports and EPIE Reports;

4) Education journals such as Educational Technology;

5) Newsletters of educational computer users groups such as the MACUL Journal;

6) Software guidebooks such as Online Micro-Software Guide & Directory;

7) Online sources through Dialog databases, e.g. Microcomputer Index.

Preview of media software is required when possible with publishers permission before purchase of the title.

N. Multiple Copies

Requests from faculty for multiple copies of books will be individually considered but, in general, the duplication of titles should be avoided. Since the main concern of the LRC is to provide support materials for the curriculum and to give all students a fair opportunity to thoroughly examine needed materials, multiple copies of certain books may be acquired in certain situations (at the discretion of the librarians and/or at the request of faculty members) vis-a-vis the Reserve Collection Guidelines.

LRC funds should not be used in acquiring multiple copies in lieu of textbooks to be purchased by students for specific courses. However, the LRC must have sufficient copies of titles which are assigned reading for classes, as defined and restricted by the Reserve Collection Guidelines.

See Also:
-Reserve Collection Guidelines (Appendix IV).

O. Paperbound Books

In general, a hardbound book is a preferable acquisition to a paperbound book. On occasion, if a significant price difference exists between a hardbound edition and a paperbound edition, the paper edition may be selected and a durable cover will be formatted, either at a bindery or most often in the LRC Technical Services Department.

Books selected which are only available in paperbound form will be acquired and, except for annual editions of reference books, will be given a plastic cover by the Technical Services Department.

P. Rare Books

The LRC will not attempt to purchase rare books, those materials that may be defined as being so old or scarce that they will seldom appear in the book markets, examples of which would include incunabula, sixteenth- and seventeenth- century imprints, American imprints before 1820, first editions, specially illustrated editions, books in fine bindings and other unique materials.

Q. Reference Collection

The LRC will maintain a reference collection that is current, authoritative, and well balanced with resource materials in all major fields of knowledge. The breadth of coverage in this collection will not be restricted to the WCC course offerings, but will include a full representation of all subjects. No quantitative minimum or maximum will be established but, within budget possibilities, titles will be acquired to provide strength in subjects currently relevant to LRC patrons.

It will be the responsibility of the reference librarians to select materials for the reference collection, based on their knowledge of books available and on the needs generated by their daily contact with LRC users.

The reference collection will include major works of bibliography in established fields of study, but holdings of lists of resources of other libraries will be representational and not extensive.

Periodic evaluation of the reference collection will occur and volumes which might offer misleading or outdated information will be withdrawn. On occasion, superseded editions will be retained along with the new edition if some contents of the former have research value.

See Also:
-Bibliographies
-Periodical Indexes and Abstracts

R. Regional Materials

Adequate materials on the subject of Michigan, southeast Michigan and Washtenaw County to support curriculum needs and instructional research will be collected. Emphasis will be on current, not retrospective sources. These materials will include reports and documents from governmental agencies and departments, statistical compilations, current and historical studies of the state, maps and atlases, and other substantive publications.

No attempt will be made to collect literary works by Michigan authors or extensive holdings of historical studies of the region or the state. Regional and state libraries specializing in Michigan history will be referred to for the satisfaction of these needs.

S. Replacement Copies

Books that are missing from the collection, declared lost by borrowers, or are too worn for further circulation are not automatically replaced. The merits of the books in question must be considered by the librarians before replacement copies are authorized. The librarian should be aware of any special demands for the missing books and should also consider if the original book has been superseded by newer and better material.

T. Reserve Collection

The reserve collection is a collection of LRC and instructor owned materials which have been separated from the larger collection (in the case of LRC materials) for restricted use. Only students enrolled in specific courses have access to materials placed on reserve and the loan period is shortened to an overnight, one-, three-day, or one-week loan or LRC use only, as specified by the instructor.

Guidelines affecting reserve items follow:

1) Only books, articles, audiovisuals, etc. that are required reading/listening for a course currently being taught should be placed on reserve.

2) Every effort should be made to restrict the number of titles (books, pamphlets, reprints, tapes, and related items) placed on reserve.

3) The ratio of 1:10 will be applied in determining the maximum number of tape copies for a given class.

4) Photocopies of copyrighted materials provided to the LRC by faculty members must comply with copyright law. It is the responsibility of the faculty member to request permission of the copyright holder to photocopy copyrighted materials.

5) Faculty must allow reasonable time for processing of materials for reserve. It is preferred by LRC staff that all reserve items be received by the LRC at least two weeks prior to the start of the semester. Exceptions will be considered only if based on sound curricular reasons.

6) The use of items placed on reserve will be annually reviewed and items which did not circulate will be removed and, if instructors' copies, will be returned to them.

See Also:
-Reserve Collection Guidelines and Procedures (Appendix IV).

U. Restriction of Materials

The Learning Resource Center will not exercise any restrictive policies on books, serials, and media software that could be construed to be a form of censorship, with the following exceptions:

1) Books placed on reserve by the faculty.

2) Materials in the College Archives and Professional Collection.

3) Books or periodicals which, because of illustrations or content are likely to be mutilated or stolen. These materials will be given the designation "Counter circulating" and will be available to patrons who request them at the circulation counter. Librarians will annually review these materials with the goal of returning these materials to open stacks if their popularity or threat of mutilation has diminished.

4) Media software shelved behind the circulation counter. Media software is cataloged and assigned an identification number. It is accessible to patrons through the use of the card catalog or the Media Catalog.

The LRC will generally maintain open stacks and will not develop special collections that have limited access or use.

See Also:
-Rare Books
-Reserve Collection Guidelines and Procedures (Appendix IV).

V. Size of the Collection

The true value and strength of a college library cannot be measured merely by the number of books held. Rather, the size of the library collection should be determined by:

1) The extent and nature of the curriculum;

2) The methods of instruction used by the faculty;

3) The size of occupational and general education student bodies with consideration of their full-time and part-time status;

4) The need of the faculty and staff for research and other advanced materials;

5) The availability of research materials in other libraries;

6) The recommended holdings levels as put forth by the American Library Association, College and Research Libraries Division standards.

VIII. GUIDELINES FOR SPECIALIZED FORMS OF MATERIALS

A. Annual Reports

The LRC will maintain a collection of annual reports in the business section of the vertical file. This collection is comprised of reports of the fifty largest American corporations as listed in the Fortune 500 report, and the reports of local and regional Michigan companies which demonstrate significant business activity. Since these reports are primarily for the use of persons interested in local employment, a few non-Michigan companies may be included if they hire locally and if their reports are requested by patrons. Both types of reports are interfiled alphabetically by name of company.

B. Bibliographies

A strong collection of subject and collective bibliographies will be acquired, the purpose being two-fold. First, through the use of bibliographical reference sources and indexes the librarians will be able to measure the depth of the collection and, second, they will be able to identify standard titles that should be acquired. The bibliographies will also provide the means of locating research materials available in other libraries through interloan service, thus augmenting the research potential on this campus immeasurably.

National, trade, comprehensive bibliographies and subject bibliographies of a specific disciplinary interest will be maintained in the Reference Collection. Although all bibliographies are generally considered to be reference works, it is the view of the reference librarians that their use (and especially the use of subject bibliographies) must be encouraged through non-restricted access. Therefore, some subject bibliographies will be housed in the general collection. As an example, the Health Sciences Information Sources will be found in the reference collection while a Guide to Library Resources in Nursing will be shelved in the general collection.

C. Campus Archival Materials

The WCC Archives are located in Room SC 355 in the LRC. An LRC librarian has responsibility for the organization, cataloging, and upkeep of the collection. A college committee appointed by the President is responsible for collection of archival materials and development of plans, policies, and a budget for the Archives.

The following files are maintained:

1. Biographies
   Biographical materials regarding trustee members, presidents, executive administrators, faculty, and college alumni.

2. Subjects
   Over 11,000 archival materials regarding college history have been organized by subject arrangement.

3. Pictures
   Photographs of college staff, students and members of the community are included in this file as well as photographs of WCC buildings and campuses.

Additional files:

1. Ann Arbor Review, 1967-1979
2. Focus, 1980-1987
3. Link-up, 1980 to date
4. Little Voice, 1970-1971
5. Minutes of the Board of Trustee meetings, 1965 to date
6. Scrapbook, 1964-
7. Voice, 1966-1978

D. Children's Books

A representative collection of children's books will be maintained to provide students of literature with the best examples of books published for children. The well-known classics in literature and the award-winning books of each year will formulate the holdings. It is not the LRC's intention to offer a full and comprehensive collection of children's books.

The reading interests will span the pre-school ages through the junior high level and will include picture books, fiction, poetry, and biographies.

Books written for high school readers that are expository in nature will be designated for the general book collection for their value as basic materials.

Selection of new titles for the juvenile collection will be made by the librarians from reviews, notable book lists, bibliographies, the Children's Catalog, and upon recommendations of faculty members.

E. Computer Programs

Microcomputer software programs which are compatible with LRC owned equipment will be acquired for the media collection. Guidelines and criteria for selection are similar to those for the selection and acquisition of other LRC media. The primary purpose is to support or enhance instruction.

Because evaluative reviews are often unavailable to selectors of computer software, additional requirements for the purchase of computer software are necessary. These are: 1) A preview copy must be requested from the vendor; 2) If a preview copy is unavailable, the item will be bought on approval and a testing mechanism will be established with the faculty requestor for determination of the quality of the program.

The LRC will abide by copyright law regarding the use and duplication of computer programs.

Computer games will be purchased if conditions exist as described under Games in this statement.

See Also:
- -Games
- -Media Selection and Acquisition Guidelines (Appendix I).
- -Learning Resource Center Guidelines on Use of Computer Software (Appendix VII).

F. Encyclopedias

Because of the high cost of sets of encyclopedias, the LRC will schedule such purchases over a period of years, replacing the oldest, well-used sets in the collection as funds permit. Encyclopedias will be maintained in the reference collection. Superseded sets will be placed in the general collection if determined to be useful for special content features; otherwise, they will be offered to other libraries.

The specialized encyclopedias of various disciplines are sought for acquisition as helpful survey material in those areas.

G. Dissertations

One copy of doctoral dissertations of WCC faculty or staff will be catalogued and housed in the Professional Collection in the LRC. Other dissertations will be purchased only in special cases for College research projects.

H. Fiction

The LRC will not buy fiction that is anticipated to have only short term interest among readers but will attempt to select new works of promise in the literary field; especially those works which would support literature course offerings. As part of the selection process librarians will evaluate the work in terms of the author's earlier writings and current reader interest.

I. Films and Film Loops

The LRC will purchase films for a permanent film collection if at least one of the following criteria is met besides the usual technical and content related selection criteria for media software:

1) The film is unavailable for rental and has been in heavy demand for at least two years; or, the rental fee is equal to the purchase price;

2) The film has been rented frequently over time, appears to be of enduring value, and its purchase price has been exceeded by rental fees;

3) The subject is best represented by the film medium and is required for adequate subject coverage in the collection.

Instructors are encouraged to avail themselves of the Instructional Media film rental service. Most films are of short term instructional value and, although the subject may remain of importance, the visuals become dated and limit effectiveness of instruction. Rental is an encouraged option.

Super 8mm film loops are an undesirable format because of storage and use considerations and will be purchased only if the content cannot be acquired in another format.

J. Games

Games that instruct through simulation may be acquired as part of the non-print collection providing that:

1) They are recommended for selection by a faculty member;

2) Authoritative evaluations of the games indicate their appropriateness and anticipated usefulness as learning devices;

3) Their continuing use can be assured;

4) The LRC will have final authority as to the processing and permanent location of the games.

Any games that require any special equipment of major proportions will not be considered.

K. Manuscripts

The LRC will generally not seek to acquire manuscripts unless that is the only format in which important materials essential to college research are available.

See Also:
-Rare Books

L. Maps

Maps of the world, of the United States, and of the region will be acquired and maintained. Selection decisions such as the type of maps needed, e.g. physical, commercial, hydrogeologic, etc. will be made by the librarians.

Attempts will be made to acquire special maps required to support the geology courses.

Maps will be cataloged for convenient access and will be stored in map cases and cabinets for their preservation.

It will be the responsibility of the librarians to replace any maps that are no longer accurate. Outdated maps should only be retained if they are of political or historical value.

M. Microforms

Micro formats generally acquired will be 35mm microfilm and microfiche. Microforms for which there is not supporting viewing equipment in the LRC will not be purchased.

Microforms will generally consist of serials, indexes, newspapers, periodically issued reports and related items, rather than monographs.

The librarians will assure that there is index (or catalog) access to materials in microforms.

See Also:
-Serials

N. Musical Scores

Musical scores or songbooks will be acquired only as necessary to represent areas such as musical or cultural history and will not be purchased as performance materials.

O. Newspapers

The LRC will seek to provide a representation of national, regional, and local publications. The choice of foreign language newspapers will be correlated primarily with those languages taught in the WCC curriculum. A diversity of political and social viewpoints should also be represented in the selection of newspapers.

Certain major newspapers, offering national or local coverage, will be maintained on microfilm, provided that full indexing is available. Other newspapers are not kept permanently but are discarded according to a retention schedule reviewed periodically by the librarians.

P. Pamphlets

Pamphlets will be selected by the same criteria of usefulness and authenticity as used for books. These materials will generally be held in the Vertical File and will be reviewed biannually for their continuing value. Since many of the pamphlets will be obtained without charge, selection of materials should follow the requirements cited for Free Materials.

The principal sources for pamphlets are:

1) U.S. Government Printing Office listings in the Monthly Catalog of Government Publications.

2) Vertical File Index.

3) Educators' Guide to Free and Inexpensive Materials.

See Also:
-Free Materials
-Commercially Sponsored Materials

Q. Periodical Indexes and Abstracts

Because access to the holdings in periodicals is possible only through the use of indexes and abstracts, it is imperative that the LRC maintains a full range of these services, representing all disciplines now included in the campus curriculum or expected to be included in the foreseeable future. The LRC collection will emphasize indexes; both the basic comprehensive indexes and those that are subject specific. New formats of indexes such as CD ROM must be considered for selection using the same evaluative criteria as print indexes for content and journal coverage. Other criteria based on the limitations, requirements, and opportunities of the new technology must be considered as well. Abstracting services considered to be of major value to faculty and students will be included in the book collection or available for access and retrieval through online bibliographic retrieval services.

These materials are valuable in both the current and retrospective research situations. Therefore, they should be maintained in current subscriptions and, whenever possible, in substantive back runs as budget limitations permit. If a useful index ceases publication, it should be retained in the Index (Reference) collection of the LRC for its value as a retrospective source.

As provided in the statement regarding the choice of serials for the LRC, a major consideration for acquisition of periodicals will be inclusion in one or more of the indexing services.

See Also:
-Reference Collection
-Serials

R. Pictures

Pictures - flat pictures, photographs, or framed art - will not systematically be acquired by the LRC. However, such materials will be collected as part of the campus archival function of the LRC. Also, picture materials that are requested by the faculty members as unique and documented needs for a specific curricular program will be considered for acquisition.

S. Recordings

Recordings, in disc and on tape, will be acquired by the library upon the recommendations of the faculty and of the media librarian. The tape format is preferred because of its durability and ease in storing, but the disc format will be selected if other factors outweigh the physical disadvantages. Recordings will be replaced as need dictates, not systematically.

Recordings will include musical composition, spoken word, literary readings, and special effects.

See Also:
-Tapes-Audio and Video

T. Serials

Serials are defined as publications which are published continuously for an indefinite period of time. Included are transactions, proceedings, annual and biannual handbooks, newspapers and a broad spectrum of publications loosely described as periodicals and journals.

A major portion of the LRC budget is regularly committed to serials, and of all library accounts serials generally experience the highest price increases annually. Since serials are subscribed to on the assumption that the LRC will continue to receive them indefinitely, the cost and handling problems inherent to serials require special care and caution in their selection.

Serials will be evaluated and selected based on the following considerations:

1) Will a title support and strengthen work in present or foreseen curricula of this campus?

2) Is the title indexed by an indexing or abstracting service held by the LRC? (Statistics indicate that only an extremely small percentage of unindexed serials is ever used by undergraduate and masters level students. Students rely on index/abstract access to serials and are generally unaware of

resources in titles not so accessed). The LRC would subscribe to an unindexed title only if:

a) The contents are so important as to assure index coverage in the very near future;

b) The contents are so timely and subject oriented as to draw wide attention to the periodical;

c) It will be heavily referred to by one or more faculty members who will be making specific class assignments requiring its use;

d) It is self contained and does not require index coverage as in the case of handbooks and some "year's work" and "progress in" publications;

e) It is a statistical reporter or provides similar information regularly relied on by students, library staff and faculty;

f) It is a book selection tool or otherwise aids the library LRC staff and/or faculty in expanding and improving library LRC collections and services.

3) The LRC will not attempt to become primarily a research facility, relying instead on four year college libraries' resources for strength in this area. In this respect, subscriptions deemed more appropriate to advanced research support than to curriculum support will not be ordered.

Serials, once placed on order, will be continued as long as budget support is available and until the curriculum changes dramatically. Titles will not be dropped capriciously to free monies for new serials.

The method of retention will be determined by the librarian after inspecting issues of the serial.

Back runs of journals will be considered on a title by title basis and, if acquired, will generally be sought in the following sequence:

1) Microfilm.

2) A complete year of paper issues of a new subscription which starts mid-year.

3) The Duplicate Exchange Union and the United States Book Exchange are options to be considered if microfilm is not available, or if a back run is not available from the publisher or vendor.

A small number of general interest periodicals may, at the discretion of the professional library staff, be added for the leisure use and enjoyment of the students at WCC or to support campus activities not directly a part of the academic curriculum.

New serial requests must be documented in writing by the person requesting same, such documents to be retained permanently on file for future references. Requests should be routed through usual acquisitions channels.

All serial requests will be reviewed by the LRC director and librarians, and final approval or rejection will be made by this group.

See Also:
-Guidelines for Selection of Periodicals (Appendix VII).

U. Sets and Series

Before agreeing to the selection of a work that is part of a finite set or an infinite series, the librarians should consider the obligations incurred. Inasmuch as certain materials in sets or series are often not separate entities and need the other volumes to be fully useful, individual titles cannot be selected without careful consideration of the acquisition of the entire set.

The serials selection statement included above describes the method by which serials, sets and series are requested and the funds committed.

See Also:
-Serials

V. Slides

Slides will be acquired by the LRC upon the recommendations of the faculty and the media librarian.

See Also:
-Media Selection Guidelines (Appendix I).

W. Tapes

Audio and/or video tapes will be acquired by the LRC upon the recommendation of faculty and the Media Librarian. Video tapes must be compatible with LRC owned equipment, available in the facility or for distribution to campus sites.

See Also:
-Media Selection Guidelines (Appendix I).

X. Textbooks

Textbooks for college courses will not be systematically acquired by the LRC. The high cost of textbooks, the incidence of frequent theft and student abuse of textbook loan privileges, their rapid obsolescence, and the lack of standardization in textbooks required for the curriculum offerings makes purchase by the LRC unwise and financially prohibitive. The LRC does permit, however, that a textbook provided by the instructional area be put on reserve for student use. A small number of textbooks if determined to be the only available source and are excellent general introductions to a subject, or surveys of a discipline, will be acquired.

Instructor's manuals, laboratory manuals, assignment workbooks for student use problem solvers, and other similar publications are generally not desirable materials to be added to the permanent collection of the LRC and, as such, will rarely be acquired.

See Also:
-Reserve Collection

Y. Videodiscs

Videodiscs will be acquired by the LRC upon recommendation of faculty and the Media Librarian. Videodiscs must be compatible with LRC owned equipment.

IX. AUDIOVISUAL PRODUCTIONS

Instructors are encouraged to participate with the Instructional Media staff in development of audiovisuals to be used in the classroom or, if appropriate, and satisfy criteria for acquisition of materials, added to the LRC media collection. The following materials can be produced in house:

1) Audiotapes
2) Laminations
3) Photographic materials
4) Transparencies
5) Slides
6) Slide/tape programs
7) Videotapes

Production requests should be delivered to the Instructional Media area, LRC.

APPENDIX I

MEDIA SELECTION AND ACQUISITION GUIDELINES

Objective: To select media materials for the Learning Resource Center collection which support instructional activities and goals at Washtenaw Community College.

Selectors: The media librarian solicits recommendations from faculty. The opinions of faculty subject experts and Instructional Media Department production staff are important in pre-order considerations. Approval to order is the responsibility of the media librarian.

Factors Influencing Selection

1. Balance and depth of the media collection must be considerations in selection.

2. The high cost of media materials requires a careful review of LRC collection strengths and weaknesses and area instructional needs before preview of an item. Effort will be made to purchase approved media as long as funds are available. When financial resources are minimal, area rotation is implemented.

3. Purchase should not be considered if rental of the item is more cost effective. Films and other videos available for rent will be purchased by the LRC, however, if frequency of use, inter-departmental need or other proven conditions justify LRC ownership.

4. Production of media inhouse is occasionally a less costly and/or faster option. Commercially produced media will be purchased when local production is not feasible.

5. Prospective audience or user of media item, for example, a group or individual students or community persons, affect the selection decision.

6. Consideration should be given to various formats when selecting media. The best format should be chosen, given the intended use of the item, the expected audience, cost factors, durability, maintenance requirements and equipment availability.

Guidelines

1. The media item must conform to the philosophies endorsed by the Library Bill of Rights (American Library Association, rev. 1980) which pertain to library materials.

Appendix I - Media Selection and Acquisition Guidelines
page 2

2. Reliable materials selection aids should be consulted before media is ordered for preview. If possible several items on the same topic should be previewed.

3. Materials should be previewed by faculty or staff requestor, media librarian, and IM production staff. It is often desirable to include students in the preview process.

4. All media should be previewed before approval to order is given. If a preview copy cannot be obtained, strong recommendations from reliable selection aids and/or evidence of the previous preview elsewhere of the entire item, e.g. the entire duration of a 16 mm films, by the requestor will be required.

5. Criteria for a thorough evaluation of the content and curricular role of the media material will be used by the previewer.

6. The material should be technically satisfactory with respect to sound, photography, narrative style, color, etc.

7. Permission to produce back-up copies of appropriate media formats will be requested by the media librarian prior to the order being placed.

Additional Requirements for the Selection of Computer Software

1. If a preview copy cannot be obtained and evaluative reviews are unavailable, the item will be bought on approval, if possible. A testing mechanism will be established with the requestor for determination of the quality of the program.

2. If permission to produce a copy of a computer program is not given by the copyright holder, the LRC will investigate purchase of a second copy at discounted price.

Related Policies and Procedures

1. LRC Book Selection Guidelines

2. Guidelines for Selection of Periodicals

3. Computer Software Evaluative Criteria

Revised February 1984

APPENDIX II

GUIDELINES FOR SELECTION OF PERIODICALS

1. The periodical collection should represent the various subjects taught at WCC in an equitable manner. There is no perfect formula for achieving a just representation of titles to correspond to the many varied subjects taught in the occupational and general studies programs. The librarian's judgment must be based on the same multiple criteria employed in book selection and she/he must be on constant guard that curricular areas are not being neglected.

2. A periodical's content should serve the student's course and informational needs as determined by the college curriculum and by library reference service.

3. A periodical's content should relate to the student's recreational and college life needs. (Since many WCC students do not use public libraries, it is necessary to include certain general interest magazines in our collection).

4. A periodical's content should serve the faculty's informational needs as they pertain to subjects taught at this institution. (Since WCC is not a research institution the LRC cannot provide materials for instructors' independent research.)

5. Unless strongly recommended by one or more instructors a new periodical will not be ordered until the librarians have examined a sample copy and judged its quality according to all relevant considerations and the guidelines.

6. A high priced periodical must be found to demonstrate superiority in terms of high demand or intrinsic worth before purchase.

7. The periodical should be indexed by at least one of the LRC's indexes to periodicals.

8. The periodical should be recommended by Katz or other authorities on magazines for libraries. (ALA Standards, 1981 should be considered for quantitative criteria).

9. Periodicals concerned with specific subject content should be presented accurately, objectively, and with documentation.

10. Objective criteria such as format, size, advertising, editor, publisher, circulation, etc. are to be considered but should not overrule a decision to purchase which is based on subjective criteria. (e.g. Some hard to read newsprint periodicals which fail above objective tests are very popular because of content and style).

11. A periodical should not violate the philosophies endorsed by the Library Bill of Rights (ALA, rev. 1980) which pertain to library materials.

APPENDIX III

GUIDELINES FOR THE ACCEPTANCE OF GIFTS

The acceptance of gifts to the Learning Resource Center will be governed by the following criteria:

1. The Learning Resource Center reserves the right to accept or reject gift items and to then catalog, display, discard or dispose of these items, as decided by the librarians responsible for selection.

2. Only gifts that support the selection objectives for the Learning Resource Center print and nonprint collections will be accepted.

3. Materials will not be accepted when a donor requires that they be kept together and not integrated into the whole Learning Resource Center collection.

4. Materials will not be accepted on an "indefinite loan."

5. Gifts frequently require more time to screen, organize, catalog and process than new material. If storage space and/or staff time are not available when gifts are offered, the Learning Resource Center may find it necessary to refuse the gifts solely on these grounds.

6. Upon the acceptance of gifts by the Learning Resource Center, the donor of library materials will receive a thank you letter from the President of Washtenaw Community College and a gift plate with the donor's name on it will be placed in each gift book catalogued for the collection. No other record of gift transactions will be kept.

7. Any appraisal for income tax purposes of a gift of books or other materials to the Learning Resource Center is the responsibility of the donor. The official acknowledgement of the gift is the thank you letter from the President; this letter does not specify prices of the materials but does specify the number of items donated.

8. The Learning Resource Center reserves the right to accept or reject any monetary gifts that restrict how and for what the money is spent, or to ask of the donor that the conditions of the gift be altered to better meet the needs of the Learning Resource Center and its patrons. Such decisions will be made by the Learning Resource Center director.

9. In those cases in which the Learning Resource Center cannot accept an offered gift, a librarian will attempt to suggest another area library which might find the material useful.

November 18, 1988 GIFTS

APPENDIX IV

RESERVE COLLECTION GUIDELINES AND PROCEDURES

Objective: To provide closer supervision and a selection of loan periods for materials in high demand by students because of their scarcity or required nature.

The reserve collection is located in the circulation area of the LRC. Materials in the collection must meet the following criteria:

1. They are REQUIRED or OPTIONAL reading for one or more courses CURRENTLY being taught.

2. They are not available in quantity.

Placing materials on reserve prohibits the general student and staff use of an item and requires considerable staff time to process materials. It is recommended, therefore, that instructors carefully consider the advisability of placing each title on reserve.

When placing materials on reserve, the following rules apply:

1. A reserve form (available at the circulation counter) must be filled out completely and accurately.

2. Reserve lists will be processed in the order received.

3. Several items will be placed on reserve at one time in so far as possible, and removed as a group. Frequent additions and removals are not recommended.

4. Library materials may be placed on reserve for one semester only.

5. Reference materials may not be placed on reserve.

6. Materials from other libraries may not be placed on reserve.

7. Instructors' materials will be processed with pockets and stickers unless requested otherwise.

8. Materials not being used by students will be withdrawn from reserve at the end of the term.

9. Textbooks may be placed on reserve only if they are not available in sufficient quantity.

10. The LRC will not be responsible for replacement of damaged or lost personal copies on reserve.

11. Material on reserve lists for which the LRC was given no removal date will be removed from reserve at the end of the term during which they were placed on reserve.

12. The ratio of 1:10 will be applied in determining the maximum number of tape copies for a given class.

13. To assure compliance with the 1978 copyright law the following rules must be observed:
    --Without written permission of the copyright holder
    a. Only one copy of any reproduced item may be placed on reserve.
    b. The source of this item must be clearly cited on the first page.
    --In the case of computer software
    a. Only originals or a legal copy will be added. Instructors may be asked to provide proof of the right to make an archival copy.

14. Computer software may be placed on reserve after the instructor has made an appointment with the microcomputer lab technician to demonstrate a program's features and use.

15. Documentation must be provided with each software package and any additional information pertinent to the assignment must be included.

16. Back-ups are to be maintained by the instuctor unless the software is being donated to the LRC collection, in which case LRC staff will assume responsibility for back-up.

17. It is highly recommended that the instructor arrange a class visit to the microcomputer lab to demonstrate the software if documentation is weak.

TYPES OF RESERVE:

CLOSED	-May only be used in the LRC.
OVERNIGHT	-Checked out at any time during the day and are due back anytime the following day.
3-DAY	-Checked out at any time during the day and are due in 3 days.
ONE-WEEK	-Checked out at any time during the day and are due in 1 week.

APPENDIX V

BOOK SELECTION GUIDELINES

In accordance with the mission of Washtenaw Community College, the primary objective of the Learning Resource Center's book selection process shall be to provide a book collection adequate to the institutional, instructional, and individual informational needs of students and staff. In meeting this objective, the librarians will pursue book selection by working closely with the faculty and seeking their advice and recommendations for purchase. Attention will also be given to book purchase recommendations from other staff and from students.

The librarians will retain the right of and responsibility for final, professional judgment on the selection of all books for inclusion in the collection. The collection will thus benefit from faculty's knowledge of their specific subject fields as well as from the librarian's knowledge of the present strengths and weaknesses of the collection. The librarians will evaluate the appropriateness of the recommended materials by consulting standard bibliographic tools and review sources and by considering the overall LRC collection development goals.

The criteria for consideration in the selection of all books, including gifts, will be based on the following points:

1. merit of the material as evidenced by accurate information, readable format, and authoritativeness in the field.
2. merit of the material compared with other available materials in the same subject area.
3. favorable evaluation of the material in the available professional selection aids.
4. where appropriate, recommendations by an authority in the subject area.

CDS_AP

THE FREEDOM TO READ

The freedom to read is essential to our democracy. It is continuously under attack. Private groups and public authorities in various parts of the country are working to remove books from sale, to censor textbooks, to label "controversial" books, to distribute lists of "objectionable" books or authors, and to purge libraries. These actions apparently rise from a view that our national tradition of free expression is no longer valid; that censorship and suppression are needed to avoid the subversion of politics and the corruption of morals. We, as citizens devoted to the use of books and as librarians and publishers responsible for disseminating them, wish to assert the public interest in the preservation of the freedom to read.

We are deeply concerned about these attempts at suppression. Most such attempts rest on a denial of the fundamental premise of democracy: that the ordinary citizen, by exercising his critical judgment, will accept the good and reject the bad. The censors, public and private, assume that they should determine what is good and what is bad for their fellow -citizens.

We trust Americans to recognize propaganda, and to reject it. We do not believe they need the help of censors to assist them in this task. We do not believe they are prepared to sacrifice their heritage of a free press in order to be "protected" against what others think may be bad for them. We believe they still favor free enterprise in ideas and expression.

We are aware, of course, that books are not alone in being subjected to efforts at suppression. We are aware that these efforts are related to a larger pattern of pressures being brought against education, the press, films, radio, and television. The problem is not only one of actual censorship. The shadow of fear cast by these pressures leads, we suspect, to an even larger voluntary curtailment of expression by those who seek to avoid controversy.

Such pressure toward conformity is perhaps natural to a time of uneasy change and pervading fear. Especially when so many of our apprehensions are directed against an ideology, the expression of a dissident idea becomes a thing feared in itself, and we tend to move against it as against a hostile deed, with suppression.

And yet suppression is never more dangerous than in such a time of social tension. Freedom has given the United States the elasticity to endure strain. Freedom keeps open the path of novel and creative solutions, and enables change to come by choice. Every silencing of a heresy, every enforcement of an orthodoxy, diminishes the toughness and resilience of our society, and leaves it the less able to deal with stress.

Now as always in our history, books are among our greatest instruments of freedom. They are almost the only means for making generally available ideas or manners of expression that can initially command only a small audience. They are the natural medium for the new idea and the untried voice from which come the original contributions to social growth. They are essential to the extended discussion which serious thought requires, and to the accumulation of knowledge and ideas into organized collections.

We believe that free communication is essential to the preservation of a free society and a creative culture. We believe that these pressures towards conformity present the danger of limiting the range and variety of inquiry and expression on which our democracy and our culture depend. We believe that every American community must jealously guard the freedom to publish and to circulate, in order to preserve its own freedom to read. We believe that publishers and librarians have a profound responsibility to give validity to that freedom to read by making it possible for the readers to choose freely from a variety of offerings.

The freedom to read is guaranteed by the Constitution. Those with faith in free men will stand firm on these constitutional guarantees of essential rights and will exercise the responsibilities that accompany these rights.

We therefore affirm these propositions:

1. It is in the public interest for publishers and librarians to make available the widest diversity of views and expressions, including those which are unorthodox or unpopular with the majority.

   Creative thought is by definition new, and what is new is different. The bearer of every new thought is a rebel until his idea is refined and tested. Totalitarian systems attempt to maintain themselves in power by the ruthless suppression of any concept which challenges the established orthodoxy. The power of a democratic system to adapt to change is vastly strengthened by the freedom of its citizens to choose widely from among conflicting opinions offered freely to them. To stifle every nonconformist idea at birth would mark the end of the democratic process. Furthermore, only through the constant activity of weighing and selecting can the democratic mind attain the strength demanded by times like these. We need to know not only what we believe but why we believe it.

2. Publishers, librarians, and booksellers do not need to endorse every idea or presentation contained in the books they make available. It would conflict with the public for them to establish their own political, moral, or aesthetic views as a standard for determining what books should be published or circulated.

   Publishers and librarians serve the educational process by helping to make available knowledge and ideas required for the growth of the mind and the increase of learning. They do not foster education by imposing as mentors the patterns of their own thought. The people should have the freedom to read and consider a broader range of ideas than those that may be held by any single librarian or publisher or government or church. It is wrong that what one man can read should be confined to what another thinks proper.

3. It is contrary to the public interest for publishers or librarians to determine the acceptability of a book on the basis of the personal history or political affiliations of the author.

   A book should be judged as a book. No art or literature can flourish if it is to be measured by the political views or private lives of its creators. No society of free men can flourish which draws up lists of writers to whom it will not listen, whatever they may have to say.

4. There is no place in our society for efforts to coerce the taste of others, to confine adults to the reading matter deemed suitable for adolescents, or to inhibit the efforts of writers to achieve artistic expression.

   To some, much of modern literature is shocking. But is not much of life itself shocking? We cut off literature at the source if we prevent writers from dealing with the stuff of life. Parents and teachers have a responsibility to prepare the young to meet the diversity of experiences in life to which they will be exposed, as they have a responsibility to help them learn to think critically for themselves. These affirmative responsibilities, not to be discharged simply by preventing them from reading works for which they are not yet prepared. In these matters taste differs, and taste cannot be legislated; nor can machinery be devised which will suit the demands of one group without limited the freedom of others.

5. It is not in the public interest to force a reader to accept with any book the prejudgment of a label characterizing the book or author as subversive or dangerous.

   The idea of labeling presupposes the existence of individuals or groups with wisdom to determine by authority what is good or bad for the citizen. It presupposes that each individual must be directed in making up his mind about the ideas he examines. But Americans do not need others to do their thinking for them.

6. It is the responsibility of publishers and librarians, as guardians of the people's freedom by individuals or groups seeking to impose their own standards or tastes upon the community at large.

   It is inevitable in the give and take of the democratic process that the political, the moral, or the aesthetic concepts of an individual or group will occasionally collide with those of another individual or group. In a free society each individual is free to determine for himself what he wishes to read, and each group is free to determine what it will recommend to its freely associated members. But no group has the right to take the law into its own hands, and to impose its own concept of politics or morality upon other members of a democratic society. Freedom is no freedom if it is accorded only to the accepted and the inoffensive.

7. It is the responsibility of publishers and librarians to give full meaning to the freedom to read by providing books that enrich the quality and diversity of thought and expression. By the exercise of this affirmative responsibility, bookmen can demonstrate that the answer to a bad book is a good one, the answer to a bad idea is a good one.

   The freedom to read is of little consequence when expended on the trivial; it is frustrated when the reader cannot obtain matter fit for his purpose. What is needed is not only the absence of restraint, but the positive provision of opportunity for the people to read the best that has been thought and said. Books are the major channel by which the intellectual inheritance is handed down, and the principal means of testing and growth. The defense of their freedom and integrity, and the enlargement of their service to society, requires of all bookmen the utmost of their faculties, and deserves of all citizens the fullest of their support.

We state these propositions neither lightly nor as easy generalizations. We here stake out a lofty claim for the value of books. We do so because we believe that they are good, possessed of enormous variety and usefulness, worthy of cherishing and keeping free. We realize that the application of these propositions may mean the dissemination of ideas and manners of expression that are repugnant to many persons. We do not state these propositions in the comfortable belief that what people read is unimportant. We believe rather that what people read is deeply important; that ideas can be dangerous; but that the suppression of ideas is fatal to a democratic society. Freedom itself is a dangerous way of life, but it is ours.

Statement issued 1953 and revised in 1972 by the American Library Association and the Association of American Publishers.

CDS_FREE

THE LIBRARY PRIVACY ACT
Act 455 of 1982

AN ACT to provide for the confidentiality of certain library records; and to provide for the selection and use of library materials.

History: 1982, Act 455, Eff. Mar. 30, 1983.

The People of the State of Michigan enact:

397.601 Short title.

Sec. 1. This act shall be known and may be cited as "the library privacy act".

History: 1982, Act 455, Eff. Mar. 30, 1983.

397.602 Definitions.

Sec. 2. As used in this act:

(a) "Library" includes a library which is established by the state; a county, city, township, village, school district, or other local unit of government or authority or combination of local units of governments and authorities; a community college district, a college or university; or any private library open to the public.

(b) "Library record" means a document, record, or other method of storing information retained by a library that identifies a person as having requested or obtained specific materials from a library. Library record does not include nonidentifying material that may be retained for the purpose of studying or evaluating the circulation of library materials in general.

History: 1982, Act 455, Eff. Mar. 30, 1983.

397.603 Library record not subject to disclosure requirements; release or disclosure of library record without consent prohibited; exception; procedure and form of written consent; hearing.

Sec. 3. (1) A library record shall not be subject to the disclosure requirements of Act No. 442 of the Public Acts of 1976, as amended, being sections 15.231 to 15.246 of the Michigan Compiled Laws.

(2) Unless ordered by a court after giving the affected library notice of the request and an opportunity to be heard thereon, a library or an employee or agent of a library shall not release or disclose a library record or portion of a library record to any person without the written consent of the person identified in that record. The procedure and form of giving written consent may be determined by the library.

(3) At a hearing conducted pursuant to subsection (2), a library may appear and be represented by counsel.

History: 1982, Act 455, Eff. Mar. 30, 1983.

397.604 Violation of § 397.603; liability; civil action; damages; attorney fees and costs.

Sec. 4. A library or an agent or employee of a library which violates section 3 shall be liable to the person identified in a record that is improperly released or disclosed. The person identified may bring a civil action for actual damages or $250.00, whichever is greater; reasonable attorney fees; and the costs of bringing the action.

History: 1982, Act 455, Eff. Mar. 30, 1983.

397.605 Selection and use of library materials.

Sec. 5. (1) Except as otherwise provided by statute or by a regulation adopted by the governing body of the library, the selection of library materials for inclusion in a library's collection shall be determined only by an employee of the library.

(2) Except as otherwise provided by law or by a regulation adopted by the governing body of the library, the use of library materials shall be determined only by an employee of the library.

History: 1982, Act 455, Eff. Mar. 30, 1983.

Route 57 West,
Washington, New Jersey 07882-9605

908-689-1090
FAX 908-689-9262

LIBRARY/LEARNING RESOURCES CENTER 908-689-7614

WARREN COUNTY COMMUNITY COLLEGE
LIBRARY/LEARNING RESOURCES CENTER

COLLECTION DEVELOPMENT POLICY

Revised May 4, 1992

TABLE OF CONTENTS

I. INTRODUCTION

The Warren County Community College Library/Learning Resources Center Collection Development Policy is designed for use as a planning tool and as a means of communicating the collection goals and policies of the Library/Learning Resources Center. The policy reflects that the Library/Learning Resources Center is constrained from accumulating all informational materials in all subject areas by limitations in funds, space and staffing. In the face of these constraints, we hope to maximize our effectiveness by establishing goals and priorities and the accompanying policies and procedures to implement them. In its function as a planning tool this collection development policy provides College and Library/Learning Resources Center decision-makers with information necessary for allocating funds for Library/Learning Resources Center materials. As a communications tool it provides the guidelines for establishing priorities for the selection of Library/Learning Resources Center materials and the criteria for the withdrawal of materials from the Library/Learning Resources Center collection. While the policies are specific, they will be interpreted as broadly as the situation may demand.

This document presents the first of a two-step process. It enumerates the collection goals of the Library/Learning Resources Center and synthesizes its policies and procedures for the selection and acquisition of different types of materials. The second step, the Collection Development Plan, provides an analysis of the collection in terms of the subjects presently represented and will detail the extent of future collecting activities in each subject area.

II. PHILOSOPHY

A primary function of education is the development in individuals of the ability to think, to understand their own and other cultures, and to be critical in the search for values and knowledge. The freedom of access to a broad spectrum of materials is critical to the development of these capabilities which are essential to our democratic way of life. Clearly, the freedom of choice in materials selection is a basic prerequisite to effective academic library service. In addition, the Library/Learning Resources Center recognizes that it shares with the teaching faculty and the administration responsibility in the instructional design of the College.

The Library/Learning Resources Center endorses the Library Bill of Rights, the Freedom to Read statement, the Freedom to View statement, the Intellectual Freedom Statement and the Professional Code of Ethics for Librarians adopted by the American Library Association as well as the Right to Read statement of the National Council of Teachers of English and the People's Library Bill of Rights adopted by the White House Conference on Library and Information Services.

III. OBJECTIVES

The primary goal of the Library/Learning Resources Center is the support of the academic programs and curricula of Warren County Community College. This is achieved through a planned, systematic acquisition program of both print and non-print information resources. In addition to the academic program, the Library/Learning Resources Center also provides support to: the goals and objectives of the College, the teaching methods of the faculty, and the goals and objectives of the Skylands Small Business Development Center.

To ensure full and appropriate use of all available resources and services, the Library/Learning Resources Center staff (professional and support) continually instruct and encourage students, faculty and clients in the use of Library/Learning Resources Center resources.

IV. SCOPE OF THE COLLECTION

The Library/Learning Resources Center is maintained for students, faculty and staff, county residents, and other clients. It serves persons with a wide range of interests, abilities and degrees of maturity. To fulfill each individual need, the Library/Learning Resources Center attempts to supply a collection of books, periodicals, pamphlets, recordings, audio-visual and other non-print materials covering all subjects relevant to the college curricula and small business needs, and seeks to present all sides of controversial issues.

The collection is composed of materials that will support classroom instruction and small business informational needs, widen the boundaries of the students' thinking, enrich their lives, and help them fulfill their recreational needs. The collection includes materials of a professional nature which aid the faculty and consultants in their teaching program and enrich professional understanding. The general reference collection includes representative works in all major fields of knowledge whether or not they are currently a part of the curriculum.

V. RESPONSIBILITY FOR COLLECTION MANAGEMENT

Responsibility for collection management for the Library/Learning Resources Center rests with the Director of the Library/Learning Resources Center. The Director may delegate to the Library/Learning Resources Center's professional staff the authority to select materials in accordance with the guidelines and objectives contained in this document. The Director keeps informed of curriculum development and the course needs of the faculty by serving on the Curriculum and Instruction Committee and through direct contact with faculty. The faculty of Warren County Community College and the Skylands Small Business Development Center are encouraged and expected to participate in the Library/Learning Resources Center's collection management program by recommending instructional materials which will support their areas of specialization. In addition, they are responsible for suggesting materials to keep the collection current and up-to-date. The Library/Learning Resources Center staff constantly seek to identify and correct inadequate coverage. Recommendations from other college staff and students are also given consideration.

VI. GENERAL POLICIES FOR MATERIALS SELECTION

The Library/Learning Resources Center recognizes that the modern library is not just a place where books are kept and read. In the midst of today's information explosion, learning occurs most effectively when all types of media--audio and video cassettes, filmstrips, transparencies, slides, microforms, periodicals, newspapers, computer software, documents, compact discs, pamphlets and books--are available and used. All of these types of materials are considered potential resources to be considered for acquisition into an organized and balanced collection. The selection of materials is a continuous process affected by the changing curriculum content and needs and the availability of new materials. The professional Library/Learning Resources Center staff uses a variety of reviewing tools to select materials. The faculty are encouraged to recommend materials reviewed in their own professional journals. The general policies for selection apply equally to all types of materials being considered for Library/Learning Resources Center acquisition.

A. General criteria for selection of all materials

1. Relevancy to the curriculum or the Skylands Small Business Development Center programs
2. Accuracy and objectivity of information
3. Strength of present holdings in the same or similar subject
4. Availability of materials on the subject through other sources
5. Authority of the author or issuing body
6. Appropriateness of the vocabulary and level of treatment to the user
7. Frequency of Interlibrary Loan requests for material on same or similar subject
8. Timeliness of material
9. Lasting value of the material
10. Coverage in indexes (particularly for periodicals and newspapers)

11. Cost
12. Physical quality of the publication (hard or soft cover, 1/2 inch or 3/4 inch tape, etc.)
13. Suitability of the specific media to the content and teaching purposes
14. Specific use of the item: instructional, professional, recreational
15. Reputation of the publisher

B. Collection Levels

Collection levels are defined within the Library/Learning Resources Center's Collection Development Plan. Most of the collection is maintained at either the instruction or teaching level or the basic level.

C. Interlibrary Loans (ILL)

It has long been apparent that no library could possibly collect all of the materials needed for use by all of its users. In order to alleviate this problem, the Library/Learning Resources Center provides an Interlibrary Loan service to all users. Through this program, most materials which have not been collected can be provided from another library. The titles and subjects of the materials borrowed through this service are carefully observed. Subjects or titles which are frequently borrowed are given priority for further evaluation and possible acquisition by the Library/Learning Resources Center.

VII. POLICIES FOR SELECTION OF SPECIFIC MATERIALS

While most selection policies apply to all types of materials, some policies and guidelines are needed for specific types of materials.

A. Textbooks

For the purposes of this policy textbooks are defined as the books and other materials adopted and required to be purchased by students for use in class. Textbooks may be included in the collection if the material presented is not available elsewhere or if the available material is too specialized for the purpose of the course. In general, textbooks are NOT systematically purchased for the collection.

B. Reference Collection

The reference collection is designed to meet both general and specific information needs. Materials covering all major fields of knowledge including those outside the realm of the curriculum should by included in the collection. The reference collection may include titles which are generally considered to be standard reference tools (encyclopedias and indexes), as well as titles which are locally regarded as reference tools because of use patterns peculiar to the Library/Learning Resources Center community (small business and careers) or because of necessity for universal availability (law and business services).

C. Research Materials

Materials needed by faculty members for research will be purchased only if they can also be used by students. Interlibrary Loan will be used to supply faculty research materials.

D. Developmental Learning Materials

Developmental learning materials are included in the collection to fulfill the needs of those students who wish to remedy weaknesses or to proceed on an individual basis in special areas.

E. Serials

For the purpose of this policy, periodicals, newspapers, and series (standing orders, annuals, reports, yearbooks, indexes, etc.) are considered serials. Because of the importance of continuity in runs, the acquisition of each serial title usually results in budgetary commitment from year to year. Because of this on-going and costly commitment in terms of annual expenses, storage and preservation, these materials are reviewed and selected with special care. Serials are reviewed on an annual basis by the professional library staff. Their recommendations for retention or cancellation are based primarily on curriculum needs, frequency of use, and budgetary considerations.

1. **Periodicals** - Periodicals (journals, magazines, etc.) are purchased to provide the most current thinking and research in the various subjects and fields; to provide information not yet available in books; to supplement and complement the book collection; for reference and research use; and to serve the staff as materials reviewing and selection tools as well as professional reading.

2. **Newspapers** - Newspapers are purchased on a current basis to meet the teaching and general informational needs of the college community. Selected titles will include domestic newspapers representing several major cities in the region, major state and local newspapers. Selection of titles will include consideration of the relevance to specific courses; current coverage of national, regional, state and local issues and events; and representation of diverse political, social and cultural viewpoints.

3. **Series** - Series are generally monographic in format but are issued in successive parts at regular intervals. Series are intended for continuous use indefinitely. Generally, though not always, these materials will be located within the reference collection. Some series, however, are more appropriate for circulation. Individual titles in a series may be acquired as separate monographs without making a commitment to place a standing order for the whole series. Because series are more expensive than other monographs, series will be selected with greater care.

4. **Preservation of Periodicals and Newspapers** - Periodicals and newspapers are selected for preservation according to the general criteria applied when the titles were originally selected for the collection. Back issues of periodicals and newspapers are valuable sources of information for users, especially students doing research. When budgetary constraints permit, periodicals and newspapers to be preserved will be obtained on microfiche and filed or bound and shelved.

F. Audio-Visual Materials

Audio-visual materials are purchased as a normal part of the Library/Learning Resources Center collection in order to provide the College community with the opportunity to learn with a variety of media. Much of the audio-visual collection is used in the classroom and is, therefore, instruction related. Whenever possible, the materials should be previewed by the library staff and at least one instructor from the related subject field. Particular attention should be paid to the quality of the product in both the physical and informational aspects. Attention should also be paid as to whether the media is appropriate for the information being presented and for the setting in which it is to be used. Audio-visual materials may be, but are not limited to, the following media:

-videocassettes
-audiocassettes
-records
-slides
-transparencies
-film strips
-compact discs
-multi-media kits

When selecting audio-visual materials priority will be given to those titles which will be integrated into a course, those titles which will be of benefit to the greatest number of students or clients, and those materials dealing with subjects not already covered by similar materials. Providing funds are available, titles will be selected which will be used as supplementary materials for courses, enrich the students lives by widening their horizons or fulfill recreational needs.

G. **Computer Software and CD-ROM**
In our ever-changing technological world, computers play an integral role. In order to prepare our students and clients, the Library/Learning Resources Center will provide a variety of computer software and programs for use in the various computer labs or Library/Learning Resources Center itself. Preference will be given to software and programs used in the curriculum or for classes. In addition, the Library/Learning Resources Center will acquire informational programs in formats conducive to student or client use, such as CD-ROM. The variety of informational materials available on CD-ROM is increasing. The Library/Learning Resources Center will make every effort to include these types of materials as permitted by budgetary considerations. Some of the products available include indexes, encyclopedias, etc.

H. **Government Documents**
The Library/Learning Resources Center is not designated as a federal or state government depository. Consequently, most government documents must be purchased. These materials are evaluated and selected according to the general policies for selection. All collected government documents are processed in the same manner as other materials. A small number of state government documents are received free of charge from the issuing government office. These materials are automatically sent to all libraries in the state at no charge.

I. **Foreign Language Materials**
In general, foreign language materials are collected only in support of the foreign language curriculum. Occasionally, a foreign language edition may be purchased when it is specifically needed or when English translations are inadequate or unavailable.

J. **New Jersey Collection**
The purpose of the New Jersey Collection is to acquire and preserve materials related to the history, geography, and culture of New Jersey and particularly Warren County. Toward this end, efforts are made to acquire such materials as they are published and to acquire out-of-print monographs on the state or county as they become available whenever budgetary constraints allow. The Library/Learning Resources Center does not, however, collect genealogies. While the major portion of the New Jersey Collection is in monograph form, the Library/Learning Resources Center also seeks to collect other types of media. The majority of the collection is housed with the main Library/Learning Resources Center collection although special storage is or will be provided for those materials which could not easily be stored in an integrated collection. All acquired materials which relate to New Jersey or Warren County are considered a part of the New Jersey collection regardless of where they are housed.

K. **College Archives**
In the absence of an official College archives, the Library/Learning Resources Center endeavors to collect and organize as many of the documentary records of the College as space and personnel constraints permit. Examples of official archival documents are: minutes of the Board of Trustees meetings; reports of the College, President, Deans, and Departmental Directors; and official files of the College administrators where available. Other official documents include minutes of the College committees and student

organizations, as well as reports and publications issued about the College by the New Jersey Department of Higher Education, accrediting bodies, etc.

The Archives Collection also includes some non-official materials relating to the facilities, students, and history of the College and to College sponsored events. Most of these materials take the form of clippings from newspapers and magazines, although appropriate materials in all types of media are accepted for inclusion in the Archives Collection. In most cases, single copies of materials are added. Duplicate copies of materials for which heavy use is anticipated may be collected.

L. Vertical File

The purpose of the vertical file is to augment other Library/Learning Resources Center collections by providing quick and easy access to pamphlets, clippings, fliers, and other ephemeral material. The emphasis in this collection is on materials covering topics of current interest and information which may be difficult to find in monograph form or which may not be contained in monographs. However, other materials for which there may be occasional or sporadic demand are also housed there.

M. Multiple Copies

The Library/Learning Resources Center will purchase multiple copies of a title if heavy and continued use of the title can be demonstrated. When an instructor expects to use a title heavily, multiple copies may be recommended. All requests for additional copies must be approved by the Director of the Library/Learning Resources Center.

N. Replacement of Irrevocably Damaged, Lost, or Stolen Materials

It is NOT the Library/Learning Resources Center's policy to routinely replace all materials because of damage or loss. The following criteria will be considered on a title-by-title basis:

1. Strength of present holdings in the same or similar subject
2. Lasting value of the material
3. Historical significance of the title
4. Availability of materials on the subject through other sources
5. Demand for the specific title or subject
6. Number of duplicate copies, if any, available
7. Availability of the specific title
8. Replacement will occur six to nine months after the loss or damage if deemed necessary. Where need for the title is imminent, replacement can be immediate.

O. Office Copies

The Library/Learning Resources Center funds are expended only for materials for which it has responsibility. The Library/Learning Resources Center will not collect resources which are exclusively for office or departmental use. Upon written request, the Library/Learning Resources Center will order these materials for other College offices and departments only with the clear understanding that said office or department must provide the funds for the purchase.

P. Gifts

Gifts of library materials are encouraged and accepted with the understanding that there are no conditions attached to their disposition. Only those materials which prove to be in good physical condition and which conform to the collection goals criteria and policies are actually added to the collection. All others are given to other libraries, sold, or discarded. All gifts are acknowledged. However, the appraisal of gifts for tax purposes is the responsibility of the donor.

VIII. COLLECTION MAINTENANCE AND EVALUATION

The Director of the Library/Learning Resources Center along with the professional Library/Learning Resources Center staff are responsible for the continuous and systematic evaluation of the collection. As with selection, the faculty is encouraged to periodically review materials in their subject area to make recommendations to the professional Library/Learning Resources staff for additional materials or withdrawals.

The withdrawal or weeding process is an integral part of the collection maintenance. Materials are withdrawn from the Library/Learning Resources Center in order to maintain a current, active, and useful collection which reflects the goals of the Library/Learning Resources Center. In addition, the shortage of space may necessitate the withdrawal of materials from the collection. In general, the criteria for selection, both general and specific, apply when considering material for withdrawal. In addition, the following criteria should be considered when evaluating items for withdrawal.

1. Superseded editions
2. Obsolescence
3. Damaged, lost, or long-overdue materials which have not been recommended for replacement
4. Appropriateness of subject matter to the collection
5. Quantity and recency of past use
6. Number of copies in the collection
7. Language in which the material is written
8. Existence of availability of indexes (particularly for periodicals and newspapers)
9. Cost of continuing subscription/standing order
10. Changes in the curriculum or Library/Learning Resources Center user population

Final decisions to withdraw are made by the professional Library/Learning Resources Center staff on a title-by-title basis.

IX. RECONSIDERATION OF LIBRARY/LEARNING RESOURCES CENTER MATERIALS

In spite of the care taken by the professional library staff and the faculty in selecting or recommending materials for inclusion in the collection, objections to a work may occasionally occur. All materials are potentially open to possible criticism. All complaints should be properly dealt with so that the complainant understands the reasoning behind the selection of the materials and so that the complainant feels his or her opinions have been listened to and given consideration. The following measures should be taken upon receipt of a complaint.

A. Registration of Complaints
   1. Complainants who come into the Library/Learning Resources Center should be politely directed to the Director of the Library/Learning Resources Center or designee.
   2. Complainants who telephone should be listened to politely and referred to the Director of the Library/Learning Resources Center or designee.
   3. Complainants who write will be called by the Director of the Library/Learning Resources Center.

B. The Director of the Library/Learning Resources Center should discuss the material and the complaint with the person objecting to it. Many complaints can be resolved simply through the personal contact of a meeting or phone call, without the need for a formal written complaint.

C. If the complainant is not satisfied with the discussion, he or she should be invited to file a formal written complaint using the Request for Reconsideration of Library Materials form.

There should be no commitments regarding action at this stage of the procedure.

D. Completed forms for reconsideration will be returned to the Director of the Library/Learning Resources Center.

E. The Director of the Library/Learning Resources Center will schedule a meeting of the Library Material Reconsideration Committee within ten days of the receipt of the complaint. The committee will be composed of the following persons:
   1. Academic Dean
   2. Director of the Library/Learning Resources Center
   3. Two faculty members (one from material's discipline or the Director of the SSBDC or designee for small business materials)
   4. One support staff member

F. The Director of the Library/Learning Resources Center will provide copies of all pertinent information with regard to the material in question, including the complaint, to committee members.

G. The complainant will receive written notification of the date and time of the scheduled meeting by registered mail.

H. The complainant must attend any and all meetings concerning the objection. Failure to attend will constitute a withdrawal of the complaint.

I. Both the complainant and the Library/Learning Resources Center staff will present information regarding the material in question to the Committee at the meeting. The Committee will issue its decision regarding said material to the Library/Learning Resources Center and the complainant based on the information they provided and committee discussion.

J. Appeals of the decision of the Library Materials Reconsideration Committee may be made to the President of the College. All appeals must be made within seven days of the decision in writing.

K. Appeals of the decision of the President may be made to the Board of Trustees. All appeals must be made within seven days of the decision in writing.

WARREN COUNTY COMMUNITY COLLEGE
LIBRARY/LEARNING RESOURCES CENTER
REQUEST FOR RECONSIDERATION OF LIBRARY/LEARNING RESOURCES CENTER MATERIALS

Title:____

Author:____

Publisher or Producer:____

Date of Publication:____

Type of Material: _____Book _____Periodical _____Videocassette
_____Audio _____Other (specify: ______________)

Request initiated by:____

Address:____

Telephone:____

Complainant Represents:
_______Himself/Herself
_______Group/Organization (please name)______________________________
Organization address______________________________

1. Have you read, viewed, or heard the **ENTIRE** work?
_____Yes _____No

2. Have you been able to discuss this work with the librarian who recommended or ordered it?
_____Yes _____No

3. To what in the material in question do you object? (Please be specific; cite pages, scenes, etc.)
____
____
____
____

4. What do you feel might be the result of using this material?
____
____
____

5. What do you understand to be the general purpose for using this work?
a. Provide support for College curriculum and programs
_____Yes _____No
b. Provide support for SSBDC programs
_____Yes _____No
c. Provide an opportunity to widen the users' thinking or enrich their lives
_____Yes _____No
d. Provide fulfillment of recreational needs
_____Yes _____No

e. Provide support and development of the teaching methods of the faculty
_____Yes _____No

6. Did the general purpose of the material, as described by the librarian, seem a suitable one to you?
_____Yes _____No
If not, please explain.____
____
____

7. What do you think is the general purpose of the author/creator of this material?
____
____
____

8. Are you aware of the professional critical judgement of this material?
_____Yes _____No

9. Would you like the librarian to give you copies of the written professional reviews about this material?
_____Yes _____No

10. Do you have negative reviews of the material?
_____Yes _____No
If so, where were they published?____
____

11. Would you be willing to provide copies of the reviews you have collected?
_____Yes _____No

12. What would you like the Library/Learning Resources Center to do about this material?
Please explain.____
____
____
____

13. If you are of the opinion that it should not be available, what material would you recommend that would convey as valuable a picture and perspective of the subject treated?______________
____
____

The undersigned complainant agrees to attend any meetings related to this complaint. Failure to attend any meeting will constitute a withdrawal of the complaint.

____
Signature of Complainant

____
Date

X. REVIEW OF THE COLLECTION DEVELOPMENT POLICY

The Collection Development Policy Statement will be reviewed periodically and revised as necessary.

XI. APPENDICES

A. Library Bill of Rights

The American Library Association affirms that all libraries are forums for information and ideas, and that the following basic policies should guide their services.

1. Books and other library resources should be provided for the interest, information, and enlightenment of all people of the community the library serves. Materials should not be excluded because of the origin, background, or views of those contributing to their creation.

2. Libraries should provide materials and information presenting all points of view on current and historical issues. Materials should not be proscribed or removed because of partisan or doctrinal disapproval.

3. Libraries should challenge censorship in the fulfillment of their responsibility to provide information and enlightenment.

4. Libraries should cooperate with all persons and groups concerned with resisting abridgment of free expression and free access to ideas.

5. A person's right to use a library should not be denied or abridged because of origin, age, background, or views.

6. Libraries which make exhibit spaces and meeting rooms available to the public they serve should make such facilities available on an equitable basis, regardless of the beliefs or affiliations of individuals or groups requesting their use.

Adopted June 18, 1948. Amended February 2, 1961, June 27, 1967, and January 23, 1980, by the ALA Council.

B. The Freedom to Read

The freedom to read is essential to our democracy. It is continuously under attack. Private groups and public authorities in various parts of the country are working to remove books from sale, to censor textbooks, to label "controversial" books, to distribute lists of "objectionable" books or authors, and to purge libraries. These actions apparently rise from a view that our national tradition of free expression is no longer valid; that censorship and suppression are needed to avoid the subversion of politics and the corruption of morals. We, as citizens devoted to the use of books and as librarians and publishers responsible for disseminating them, wish to assert the public interest in the preservation of the freedom to read.

We are deeply concerned about these attempts a suppression. Most such attempts rest on a denial of the fundamental premise of democracy: that the ordinary citizen by exercising his critical judgment, will accept the good and reject the bad. The censors, public and private, assume that they should determine what is good and what is bad for their fellow-citizens.

We trust Americans to recognize propaganda, and to reject it. We do not believe they need the help of censors to assist them in this task. We do not believe they are prepared to sacrifice their heritage of a free press in order to be "protected" against what others think may be bad for them. We believe they still favor free enterprise in ideas and expression.

We are aware, of course, that books are not alone in being subjected to efforts at suppression. We are aware that these efforts are related to a larger pattern of pressures being brought against education, the press, films, radio, and television. The problem is not only one of actual censorship. The shadow of fear cast by these pressures leads, we suspect, to an even larger voluntary curtailment of expression by those who seek to avoid controversy.

Such pressure toward conformity is perhaps natural to a time of uneasy change and pervading fear. Especially when so many of our apprehensions are directed against an ideology, the expression of a dissident idea becomes a thing feared, in itself, and we tend to move against it as against a hostile deed, with suppression.

And yet suppression is never more dangerous than in such a time of social tension. Freedom has given the United States the elasticity to endure strain. Freedom keeps open the path of novel and creative solutions, and enables change to come by choice. Every silencing of a heresy, every enforcement of an orthodoxy, diminishes the toughness and resilience of our society and leaves it the less able to deal with stress.

Now as always in our history, books are among our greatest instruments of freedom. They are almost the only means for making generally available ideas or manners of expression that can initially command only a small audience. They are the natural medium for the new idea and the untried voice from which come the original contributions to social growth. They are essential to the extended discussion which serious thought requires, and to the accumulation of knowledge and ideas into organized collections.

We believe that free communication is essential to the preservation of a free society and a creative culture. We believe that these pressures towards conformity present the danger of limiting the range and variety of inquiry and expression on which our democracy and our culture depend. We believe that every American community must jealously guard the freedom to publish and to circulate, in order to preserve its own freedom to read. We believe that publishers and librarians have a profound responsibility to give validity to that freedom to read by making it possible for the readers to choose freely from a variety of offerings.

The freedom to read is guaranteed by the Constitution. Those with faith in free men will stand firm on these constitutional guarantees of essential rights and will exercise the responsibilities that accompany these rights.
We therefore affirm these propositions:

1. It is in the public interest for publishers and librarians to make available the widest diversity of views and expressions, including those which are unorthodox or unpopular with the majority.

   Creative thought is by definition new, and what is new is different. The bearer of every new thought is a rebel until his idea is refined and tested. Totalitarian systems attempt to maintain themselves in power by the ruthless suppression of any concept which challenges the established orthodoxy. The power of a democratic system to adapt to change is vastly strengthened by the freedom of its citizens to choose widely from among conflicting opinions offered freely to them. To stifle every nonconformist idea at birth would mark the end of the democratic process. Furthermore, only through the constant activity of weighing and selecting can the democratic mind attain the strength demanded by times like these. We need to know not only what we believe but why we believe it.

2. Publishers, librarians, and booksellers do not need to endorse every idea or presentation contained in the books they make available. It would conflict with the public interest for them to establish their own political, moral, or aesthetic views as a standard for determining what books should be published or circulated.

   Publishers and librarians serve the educational process by helping to make available knowledge and ideas required for the growth of the mind and the increase of learning. They do not foster education by imposing as mentors the patterns of their own thought. The people should have the freedom to read and consider a broader range of ideas than those that may be held by any single librarian or publisher or government or church. It is wrong that what one man can read should be confined to what another thinks proper.

3. It is contrary to the public interest for publishers or librarians to determine the acceptability of a book on the basis of the personal history or political affiliations of the author.

   A book should be judged as a book. No art or literature can flourish if it is to be measured by the political views or private lives of its creators. No society of free men can flourish which draws up lists of writers to whom it will not listen, whatever they may have to say.

4. There is no place in our society for efforts to coerce the taste of others, to confine adults to the reading matter deemed suitable for adolescents, or to inhibit the efforts of writers to achieve artistic expression.

   To some, much of modern literature is shocking. But is not much of life itself shocking? We cut off literature at the source if we prevent writers from dealing with the stuff of life. Parents and teachers have a responsibility to prepare the young to meet the diversity of experiences in life to which they will be exposed, as they have a responsibility to help them learn to think critically for themselves. These are affirmative responsibilities, not to be discharged simply by preventing them from reading works for which they are not yet prepared. In these matters taste differs, and taste cannot be legislated; nor can machinery be devised which will suit the demands of one group without limiting the freedom of others.

5. It is not in the public interest to force a reader to accept with any book the prejudgment of a label characterizing the book or author as subversive or dangerous.

The idea of labeling presupposes the existence of individuals or groups with wisdom to determine by authority what is good or bad for the citizen. It presupposes that each individual must be directed in making up his mind about the ideas he examines. But Americans do not need others to do their thinking for them.

6. It is the responsibility of publishers and librarians, as guardians of the people's freedom to read, to contest encroachments upon that freedom by individuals or groups seeking to impose their own standards or tastes upon the community at large.

   It is inevitable in the give and take of the democratic process that the political, the moral, or the aesthetic concepts of an individual or group will occasionally collide with those of another individual or group. In a free society each individual is free to determine for himself what he wishes to read, and each group is free to determine what it will recommend to its freely associated members. But no group has the right to take the law into its own hands, and to impose its own concept of politics or morality upon other members of a democratic society. Freedom is no freedom if it is accorded only to the accepted and the inoffensive.

7. It is the responsibility of publishers and librarians to give full meaning to the freedom to read by providing books that enrich the quality and diversity of thought and expression. By the exercise of this affirmative responsibility, bookmen can demonstrate that the answer to a bad book is a good one, the answer to a bad idea is a good one.

   The freedom to read is of little consequence when expended on the trivial; it is frustrated when the reader cannot obtain matter fit for his purpose. What is needed is not only the absence of restraint, but the positive provision of opportunity for the people to read the best that has been thought and said. Books are the major channel by which the intellectual inheritance is handed down, and the principal means of its testing and growth. The defense of their freedom and integrity, and the enlargement of their service to society, requires of all bookmen the utmost of their faculties, and deserves of all citizens the fullest of their support.

   We state these propositions neither lightly nor as easy generalizations. We here stake out a lofty claim for the value of books. We do so because we believe that they are good, possessed of enormous variety and usefulness, worthy of cherishing and keeping free. We realize that the application of these propositions may mean the dissemination of ideas and manners of expression that are repugnant to many persons. We do not state these propositions in the comfortable belief that what people read is unimportant. We believe rather that what people read is deeply important; that ideas can be dangerous; but that the suppression of ideas is fatal to a democratic society. Freedom itself is a dangerous way of life, but it is ours.

This statement was originally issued in May 1953 by the Westchester Conference of the American Library Association and the American Book Publishers Council, which in 1970 consolidated with the American Educational Publishers Institute to become the Association of American Publishers.

Adopted June 25, 1953. Revised January 28, 1972, by the ALA Council.

C. Freedom to View

The FREEDOM TO VIEW, along with the freedom to speak, to hear, and to read, is protected by the First Amendment to the Constitution of the United States. In a free society, there is no place for censorship of any medium of expression. Therefore, we affirm these principles:

1. It is in the public interest to provide the broadest possible access to films and other audiovisual materials because they have proven to be among the most effective means for the communication of ideas. Liberty of circulation is essential to ensure the constitutional guarantee of freedom of expression.

2. It is in the public interest to provide for our audiences, films and other audiovisual materials which represent a diversity of views and expression. Selection of a work does not constitute or imply agreement with or approval of the content.

3. It is our professional responsibility to resist the constraint of labeling or pre-judging a film on the basis of the moral, religious, or political beliefs of the producer or filmmaker or on the basis of controversial content.

4. It is our professional responsibility to contest vigorously, by all lawful means, every encroachment upon the public's freedom to view.

This statement was originally drafted by the Educational Film Library Association's Freedom to View Committee, and was adopted by the EFLA Board of Directors in February, 1979. Libraries and educational institutions are encouraged to adopt this statement and display it in their catalogs or libraries. The text of the statement may be reprinted freely; permission is granted to all educational institutions to use it.

Adopted by the Council, American Library Association, June 1979.

D. Intellectual Freedom Statement

An Interpretation of the Library Bill of Rights

The heritage of free men is ours.

In the Bill of Rights to the United States Constitution, the founders of our nation proclaimed certain fundamental freedoms to be essential to our form of government. Primary among these is the freedom of expression, specifically the right to publish diverse opinions and the right to unrestricted access to those opinions. As citizens committed to the full and free use of all communications media and as professional persons responsible for making the content of those media accessible to all without prejudice, we, the undersigned, wish to assert the public interest in the preservation of freedom of expression.

Through continuing judicial interpretations of the First Amendment to the United States Constitution, freedom of expression has been guaranteed. Every American who aspires to the success of our experiment in democracy--who has faith in the political and social integrity of free men--must stand firm on those Constitutional guarantees of essential rights. Such Americans can be expected to fulfill the responsibilities implicit in those rights.

We, therefore, affirm these propositions:

1. We will make available to everyone who needs or desires them the widest possible diversity of views and modes of expression, including those which are strange, unorthodox or unpopular.

   Creative thought is, by its nature, new. New ideas are always different and, to some people, distressing and even threatening. The creator of every new idea is likely to be regarded as unconventional--occasionally heretical--until his idea is first examined, then refined, then tested in its political, social or moral applications. The characteristic ability of our governmental system to adapt to necessary change is vastly strengthened by the option of the people to choose freely from among conflicting opinions. To stifle nonconformist ideas at their inception would be to end the democratic process. Only through continuous weighing and selection from among opposing views can free individuals obtain the strength needed for intelligent, constructive decisions and actions. In short, we need to understand not only what we believe, but why we believe as we do.

2. We need not endorse every idea contained in the materials we produce and make available.

   We serve the educational process by disseminating the knowledge and wisdom required for the growth of the mind and the expansion of learning. For us to employ our own political, moral, or aesthetic views as standards for determining what materials are published or circulated conflicts with the public interest. We cannot foster true education by imposing on others the structure and content of our own opinions. We must preserve and enhance the people's right to a broader range of ideas than those held by any librarian or publisher or church or government. We hold that it is wrong to limit any person to those ideas and that information another believes to be true, good, and proper.

3. We regard as irrelevant to the acceptance and distribution of any creative work the personal history or political affiliations of the author or others responsible for it or its publication.

   A work of art must be judged solely on its own merits. Creativity cannot flourish if its appraisal and acceptance by the community is influenced by the political views or private lives of the artists or the creators. A society that allows blacklists to be compiled and used to silence writers and artists cannot exist as a free society.

4. With every available legal means, we will challenge laws or governmental action restricting or prohibiting the publication of certain materials or limiting free access to such materials.
   Our society has no place for legislative efforts to coerce the taste of its members, to restrict adults to reading matter deemed suitable only for children, or to inhibit the efforts of creative persons in their attempts to achieve artistic perfection. When we prevent serious artists from dealing with truth as they see it, we stifle creative development of our children--parents, teachers, religious leaders, scientists, philosophers, statesmen--must assume the responsibility for preparing young people to cope with life as it is and to face the diversity of experience to which they will be exposed as they mature. This is an affirmative responsibility that cannot be discharged easily, certainly not with the added burden of curtailing one's access to art, literature, and opinion. Tastes differ. Taste, like morality, cannot be controlled by government, for governmental action, devised to suit the demands of one group, thereby limits the freedom of all others.

5. We oppose labeling any work of literature or art, or any persons responsible for its creation, as subversive, dangerous, or otherwise undesirable.
   Labeling attempts to predispose users of the various media of communication, and to ultimately close off a path to knowledge. Labeling rests on the assumption that persons exist who have a special wisdom, and who, therefore, can be permitted to determine what will have good and bad effects on other people. But freedom of expression rests on the premise of ideas vying in the open marketplace for acceptance, change, or rejection by individuals. Free men choose this path.

6. We, as guardians of intellectual freedom, oppose and will resist every encroachment upon the freedom by individuals or groups, private or official.
   It is inevitable in the give-and-take of the democratic process that the political, moral and aesthetic preferences of a person or group will conflict occasionally with those of others. A fundamental premise of our free society is that each citizen is privileged to decide those opinions to which he will adhere or which he will recommend to the members of a privately organized group or association. But no private group may usurp the law and impose its own political or moral concepts upon the general public. Freedom cannot be accorded only to selected groups for it is then transmuted into privilege and unwarranted license.

7. Both as citizens and professionals, we will strive by all legitimate means open to us to be relieved of the threat of personal, economic, and legal reprisals resulting from our support and defense of the principles of intellectual freedom.
   Those who refuse to compromise their ideals in support of intellectual freedom have often suffered dismissals from employment, forced resignations, boycotts of products and establishments, and other invidious forms of punishment. We perceive the admirable, often lonely, refusal to succumb to threats of punitive action as the highest form of true professionalism: dedication to the cause of intellectual freedom and the preservation of vital human and civil liberties.

   In our various capacities, we will actively resist incursions against the full exercise of our professional responsibility for creating and maintaining an intellectual environment which fosters unrestrained creative endeavor and true freedom of choice and access for all members of the community.

   We state these propositions with conviction, not as easy generalizations. We advance a noble claim for the value of ideas, freely expressed, as embodied in books and other kinds of communications. We do this in our belief that a free intellectual climate fosters creative endeavors capable of enormous variety, beauty, and usefulness, and thus worthy of support and preservation. We recognize that application of these propositions may encourage the dissemination of ideas and forms of expression that will be frightening or abhorrent to some. We believe that what people read, view, and hear is a critically important issue. We recognize, too, that ideas can be dangerous. It may be, however, that they are effectually dangerous only when opposing ideas are suppressed. Freedom, in its many facets, is a precarious course. We espouse it heartily.

Adopted by the ALA Council, June 25, 1971, Endorsed by the FREEDOM TO READ FOUNDATION, Board of Trustees, June 18, 1971.

E. Professional Code of Ethics for Librarians

1. Librarians must provide the highest level of service through appropriate and usefully organized collections, fair and equitable circulation and service policies, and skillful, accurate, unbiased, and courteous responses to all requests for assistance.

2. Librarians must resist all efforts by groups or individuals to censor library materials.

3. Librarians must protect each user's right to privacy with respect to information sought or received, and materials consulted, borrowed, or acquired.

4. Librarians must adhere to the principles of due process and equality of opportunity in peer relationships and personnel actions.

5. Librarians must distinguish clearly in their actions and statements between their personal philosophies and attitudes and those of an institution or professional body.

6. Librarians must avoid situations in which personal interests might be served or financial benefits gained at the expense of library users, colleagues, or the employing institution.

Adopted June 30, 1981, by American Library Association Membership and American Library Association Council.

F. The Right to Read

1. An open letter to the citizens of our country from the National Council of Teachers of English

> Where suspicion fills the air and holds scholars in line for fear of their jobs, there can be no exercise of the free intellect....A problem can no longer be pursued with impunity to its edges. Fear stalks the classroom. The teacher is no longer a stimulant to adventurous thinking; she becomes instead a pipe line for safe and sound information. A deadening dogma takes the place of free inquiry. Instruction tends to become sterile; pursuit of knowledge is discouraged; discussion often leaves off where it should begin.
>
> Justice William O. Douglas,
> United States Supreme Court:
> Adler v. Board of Education, 1952.

The right to read, like all rights guaranteed or implied within our constitutional tradition, can be used wisely or foolishly. In many ways, education is an effort to improve the quality of choices open to all students. But to deny the freedom of choice in fear that it may be unwisely used is to destroy the freedom itself. For this reason, we respect the right of individuals to be selective in their own reading. But for the same reason, we oppose efforts of individuals or groups to limit the freedom of choice of others or to impose their own standards or tastes upon the community at large.

The right of any individual not just to read but to read whatever he or she wants to read is basic to a democratic society. This right is based on an assumption that the educated possess judgment and understanding and can be trusted with the determination of their own actions. In effect, the reader is freed from the bonds of chance. The reader is not limited by birth, geographic location, or time, since reading allows meeting people, debating philosophies, and experiencing events far beyond the narrow confines of an individual's own existence.

In selecting books for reading by young people, English teachers consider the contribution which each work may make to the education of the reader, its aesthetic value, its honesty, its readability for a particular group of students, and its appeal to adolescents. English teachers, however, may use different works for different purposes. The criteria for choosing a work to be read by an entire class are somewhat different from the criteria for choosing works to be read by small groups. For example, a teacher might select John Knowles' A Separate Peace for reading by an entire class, partly because the book has received wide critical recognition, partly because it is relatively short and will keep the attention of many slow readers, and partly because it has proved popular with many students of widely differing abilities. The same teacher, faced with the responsibility of choosing or recommending books for several small groups of students, might select or recommend books as different as Nathaniel Hawthorne's The Scarlet Letter, Jack Schafer's Shane, Alexander Solzhenitsyn's One Day in the Life of Ivan Denisovitch, Pierre Boulle's The Bridge Over the River Kwai, Charles Dickens' Great Expectations, or Paul Zindel's The Pigman, depending upon the abilities and interests of the students in each group. And the criteria for suggesting books to individuals or for recommending something worth reading for a student who casually stops by after class are different from selecting material for a class or group. But the teacher selects, not censors, books. Selection implies that a teacher is free to choose this or that work, depending upon the purpose to be achieved and the student or class in question, but a book selected this year may be ignored next year, and the reverse. Censorship implies that certain works are not open to selection, this year or any year.

Wallace Stevens once wrote, "Literature is the better part of life. To this it seems inevitably necessary to add, provided life is the better part of literature." Students and parents have the right to demand that education today keep students in touch with the reality of the world outside the classroom. Much of classic literature asks questions as valid and significant today as when the literature first appeared, questions like "What is the nature of humanity?" "Why do people praise individuality and practice conformity?" "What do people need for a good life?" and "What is the nature of the good person?" But youth is the age of revolt. To pretend otherwise is to ignore a reality made clear to young people and adults alike on television and radio, in newspapers and magazines. English teachers must be free to employ books, classic or contemporary, which do not lie to the young about the perilous but wonderous times we live in, books which talk of the fears, hopes, joys, and frustrations people experience, books about people not only as they are but as they can be. English teachers forced through the pressures of censorship to use only safe or antiseptic works are placed in the morally and intellectually untenable position of lying to their students about the nature and condition of mankind.

The teacher must exercise care to select or recommend works for class reading and group discussion. One of the most important responsibilities of the English teacher is developing rapport and respect among students. Respect for the uniqueness and potential of the individual, an important facet of the study of literature, should be emphasized in the English class. Literature classes should reflect the cultural contributions of many minority groups in the United States, just as they should acquaint students with contributions from the peoples of Asia, Africa, and Latin America.

2. The Threat to Education

Censorship leaves students with an inadequate and distorted picture of the ideals, values, and problems of their culture. Writers may often represent their culture, or they may stand to the side and describe and evaluate that culture. Yet partly because of censorship or the fear of censorship, many writers are ignored or inadequately represented in the public schools, and many are represented in anthologies not by their best work but by their "safest" or "least offensive" work.

The censorship pressures receiving the greatest publicity are those of small groups who protest the use of a limited number of books with some "objectionable" realistic elements, such as Brave New World, Lord of the Flies, Catcher in the Rye, Johnny Got His Gun, Catch-22, Soul on Ice, or A Day No Pigs Would Die. The most obvious and immediate victims are often found among our best and most creative English teachers, those who have ventured outside the narrow boundaries of conventional texts. Ultimately, however, the real victims are the students, denied the freedom to explore ideas and pursue truth wherever and however they wish.

Great damage may be done by book committees appointed by national or local organizations to pore over anthologies, texts, library books, and paperbacks to find passages which advocate, or seem to advocate, causes or concepts or practices these organizations condemn. As a result, some publishers, sensitive to possible objections, carefully exclude sentences or selections that might conceivably offend some group, somehow, sometime, somewhere.

3. The Community's Responsibility

American citizens who care about the improvement of education are urged to join students, teachers, librarians, administrators, boards of education, and professional and scholarly organizations in support of the students' right to read. Only widespread and informed support in every community can assure that:

> enough citizens are interested in the development and maintenance of a superior school system to guarantee its achievement;
>
> malicious gossip, ignorant rumors, and deceptive letters to the editor will not be circulated without challenge and correction;
>
> newspapers will be convinced that the public sincerely desires objective school news reporting, free from slanting or editorial comment which destroys confidence in and support for schools;
>
> the community will not permit its resources and energies to be dissipated in conflicts created by special interest groups striving to advance their ideologies or biases; and
>
> faith in democratic traditions and processes will be maintained.

Adopted 1972. Updated 1982 by the National Council of Teachers of English.

G. The People's Library Bill of Rights

1. All people are entitled to free access to the information and services offered by libraries.
2. All people are entitled to obtain current and accurate information on any topic.
3. All people are entitled to courteous, efficient and timely service.
4. All people are entitled to assistance by qualified library personnel.
5. All people are entitled to the right of confidentiality in all of their dealings with libraries and librarians.
6. All people are entitled to full access to and service from library networks on local, state, regional and national levels.
7. All people are entitled to the use of a library facility that is accessible, functional and comfortable.
8. All people are entitled to be provided with a statement of the policies governing the use and services of libraries.
9. All people are entitled to library services that reflect the interests and needs of the community.

Adopted by the White House Conference on Library and Information Services, 1991.

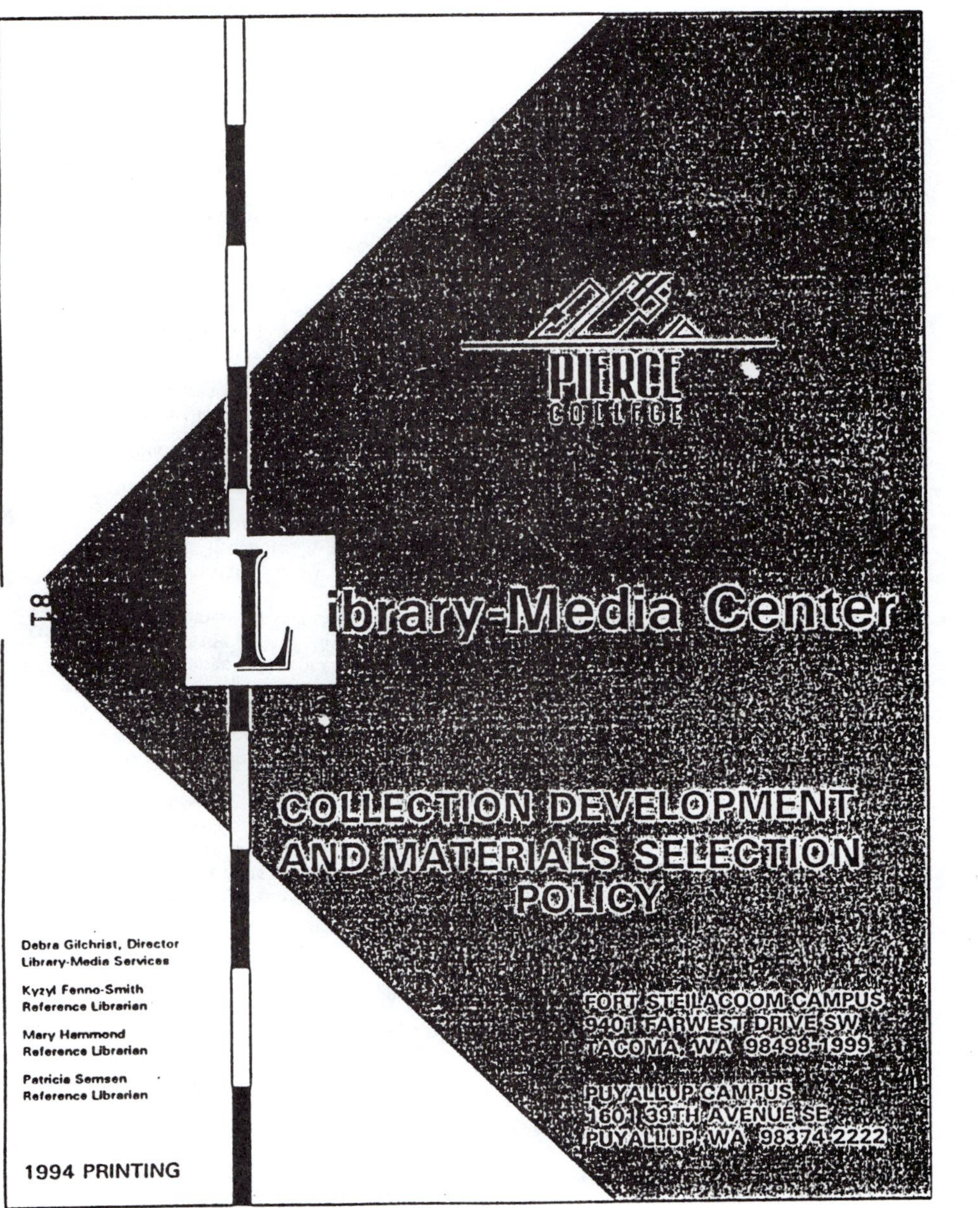

PIERCE COLLEGE

Library-Media Center

COLLECTION DEVELOPMENT AND MATERIALS SELECTION POLICY

Debra Gilchrist, Director
Library-Media Services

Kyzyl Fenno-Smith
Reference Librarian

Mary Hammond
Reference Librarian

Patricia Semsen
Reference Librarian

FORT STEILACOOM CAMPUS
9401 FARWEST DRIVE SW
TACOMA, WA 98498-1999

PUYALLUP CAMPUS
1601 39TH AVENUE SE
PUYALLUP, WA 98374-2222

1994 PRINTING

TABLE OF CONTENTS

SELECTION POLICY

PIERCE COLLEGE LIBRARY
Fort Steilacoom & Puyallup Campuses

COLLECTION DEVELOPMENT AND MATERIALS SELECTION POLICY

I. STATEMENT OF PURPOSE AND GOALS

A. Introduction

Through collections, instruction, facilities and services, the campus libraries provide leadership and support for the curricular and intellectual information needs of the college community.

Collection development is the means by which the Pierce College Library provides organized collections of print and non-print resources that will meet institutional requirements, as well as the cultural and recreational needs of the college community. Collection development is achieved by librarians, faculty, administrators, staff and students working together to select library materials which best fulfill these needs.

This policy is intended to guide the building and enrichment of the collection in accordance with the missions of Pierce College and the Pierce College Library by stating the guidelines and principles with which the process of selecting and acquiring materials will proceed. It has been developed so that available resources can be focused on those policies, practices and procedures that best enable the Pierce College Library to support the mission of the college. To accommodate internal changes in curriculum and external changes in society, it will be regularly reviewed. This policy will:

- Ensure that the library develops a collection that is responsive to the curriculum, balanced intellectually and responsive to the needs and use patterns of faculty, students and staff.
- Provide objective criteria for selection and development.
- Provide a means of interpreting the collection to potential users.
- Ensure that available resources can be focused on those policies, practices and procedures that best enable the library to support the college mission.
- Ensure that the library supports the Library Bill of Rights of the American Library Association and other principles and ideals of intellectual freedom.

II. PIERCE COLLEGE MISSION STATEMENT

Pierce College is a community college dedicated to providing academic transfer, vocational, retraining, developmental and continuing education opportunities for our students and community. As an educational institution we will maintain a strong presence within our external community and respond to the changing demographics of the 21st century. In pursuing these goals, Pierce College is strongly committed to the principles of affirmative action by providing equal opportunities in educational and occupational pursuits.

III. LIBRARY MISSION STATEMENT

It is the mission of the Pierce College Library to be a dynamic, high-quality teaching library through active and effective participation in the instructional and community service processes of Pierce College. The library will fulfill this mission by:

- Employing professionally qualified librarians who are active educators and faculty members.
- Providing maximum access to information resources and services that support and augment the classroom experience and that foster academic excellence through the freedom of inquiry.
- Encouraging and facilitating intellectual independence and lifelong learning through instructional programs and services that emphasize information competency and complement classroom instruction.
- Providing distinctive programs and services designed to meet the intellectual and cultural needs of an information-based society.
- Providing an atmosphere and environment that supports the use of information in learning and study.
- Utilizing available and emerging technologies that support and enhance instruction and information retrieval.

IV. COLLECTION OVERVIEW

A. Collection Goals

The Fort Steilacoom and Puyallup campus libraries operate collaboratively and cooperatively; the collections combine to support the entire curriculum and to form the Pierce College Library. Funds are maximized through joint collection development, low duplication of titles, rotating standing orders, and full resource sharing.

While interlibrary loan and other cooperative agreements may provide some materials needed by the college community, the libraries must receive adequate support from the institution to ensure that they will be the primary resource for the majority of the college's information needs. Materials for which there are legitimate recurring needs should be purchased by the library.

In developing and maintaining the Library's collections, the faculty librarians will be mindful of the tremendous diversity of the college's constituency. Librarians will attempt to meet the information needs of a wide variety of users, considering diversities such as ethnic/racial/national origins, religious traditions, economic backgrounds, sexual orientations, family configurations, ages, political persuasions, disabilities and learning styles.

Fort Steilacoom Campus Library

The library's collection consists of books, audio-visual materials, periodicals, digital information, pamphlets, microforms and other appropriate materials carefully selected to meet the information needs of all users. The library will strive to meet at least minimum accreditation standards in regard to collections as set forth by the Association of College and Research Libraries in Standards for Community, Junior and Technical College Learning Resources Programs (Appendix L). Attention will also be given to developing a collection that reflects and supports the cultural diversity of the college and the student body, as well as that of the greater community.

Priorities are:

1. A collection that directly supports the college curriculum through the two-year or certificate level, including audio-visual material for classroom use.
2. A collection that covers most subjects at a basic level to stimulate intellectual curiosity and allow for the pursuit of interests outside of the curriculum.
3. A collection that includes information beyond the basic level on some subjects outside of the curriculum, such as local information.

Puyallup Campus Library

The library's collection consists of books, audio-visual materials, digital information, pamphlets, microforms and other appropriate materials carefully selected to meet basic student information needs. The Puyallup campus relies heavily on the Fort Steilacoom campus for library support and will continue to do so until 1996 when the new campus library opens.

Until that time, priorities are:

1. Electronic access to the Fort Steilacoom collection, and timely document delivery.
2. Electronic, CD-ROM and paper periodical indexes that directly support the campus curriculum.
3. A reference collection that provides some breadth, but primarily focuses on materials that directly respond to faculty assignments.
4. A periodicals collection that provides some materials for general reading, but primarily focuses on journals and magazines that directly respond to faculty assignments.
5. A minimal monographic collection. Due to limited space, monographs will be de-emphasized. Monographs will be the first to be weeded or stored off-site in anticipation of the opening of the new campus library.

Emphasis at the Puyallup campus library will be on materials for service to students. In most cases, the Fort Steilacoom library assumes responsibility for services not currently available in the Puyallup campus library. However, to avail themselves of all college library services, students, faculty and staff may be expected to travel to the Fort Steilacoom campus.

B. Collection Organization

The library collections shall be organized so as to permit the most efficient access. Special collections within the library will be kept to a minimum, and will be established only after a distinct need has been identified. Special collections shall not be created through labeling; the library supports the 1990 revision of the Statement on Labeling of the ALA (Appendix F). Decisions regarding special collections shall be made by the Director of Library/Media Services and faculty librarians. Special collections currently include Paperback, Reference, Vertical File, Children's Literature, New Reader, Annual Reports, and Reserve. Special collections in areas of the college outside of the library will be discouraged so as to maximize college resources and availability of materials to students. Such collections must be approved by the Executive Dean of Instruction in consultation with the department and the Director of Library/Media Services.

Circulation, security systems and procedures must provide for both reasonable use of materials by individuals and the availability of those materials to other members of the college community who might wish to use them. Extensive circulation periods to individual patrons that may effectively result in loss of ownership of these materials, as well as overly restrictive circulation periods that unnecessarily deprive patrons of access to materials, should be avoided.

Materials needed for specific courses can be maintained in the Reserve collection that offers limited circulation on a quarter-to-quarter basis. As a general rule, Reference books will not be placed on reserve.

If material is paid for by library funds, it must remain library property and under library control. If material is loaned on a long-term basis, it must be available for immediate recall.

C. Community Served

Users are defined as students, faculty and staff of Pierce College. Although some adult Pierce County residents are granted use of the library collections and circulation privileges, the collection will not be developed, organized, or designed for their use. Faculty will not be supported in regard to individual research or material needed to prepare lectures or class presentations. Faculty research is, however, supported by the library through the provision of services such as interlibrary loan, reference assistance and database searching.

D. Cooperation Efforts

The Pierce College Libraries are committed to cooperative efforts with other area libraries, including school, college and public libraries. Every effort will be made to acquaint these libraries with Pierce College's collection development policy, and to coordinate when feasible. The Director of Library/Media Services will act as a liaison with other libraries in this endeavor. Current cooperative efforts include:

1. Biznet: Pierce College Libraries are collaborating with Pierce County Library, Tacoma Public Library and Tacoma Community College Library in supporting small business academic programs and small business owners in the community through materials, training and reference assistance. Funds are provided through the Washington State Library by the U.S. Department of Education Library Services and Construction Act.

2. Community/Technical Colleges: Reciprocal borrowing privileges are granted by all Washington State community college libraries to all currently enrolled Washington State community college students.

3. Western State Hospital: Borrowing privileges are granted to all Pierce College students and staff for use of the hospital library. All staff of Western State Hospital are granted the same use of the Pierce College Libraries. Borrowing privileges do not extend to hospital patients.

4. Interlibrary Loan: Pierce College has endorsed the Washington State Interlibrary Loan Code and provides full interlibrary loan service for all registered students, staff and faculty.

V. SELECTION

A. Responsibility for Selection

Selection and collection development are the ultimate responsibilities of the Director of Library/Media Services, who has final authority, and who authorizes the faculty librarians to carry out these obligations. These duties are fulfilled in accordance with the objectives and criteria defined in this policy. As curriculum is the most important influence on the development of the collection, it is imperative that librarians obtain suggestions and advice about materials selection from faculty and administrators and keep abreast of all changes in college curriculum. Instructors have the responsibility of recommending purchases consistent with their curricular offerings, and for considering and arranging for collection support when the college institutes new programs. Recommendations are always welcome from students, faculty, staff and community members.

Faculty librarians remain current with curricular changes by attending division meetings, consulting with other faculty members, and reviewing all course changes and proposals approved by the Council for Academic Affairs.

B. Collection Development Priorities

In establishing priorities for collection development, first consideration is given to instructional collections. Instructional collections correspond to college curriculum and directly support course and program goals. Attention is paid to the connections between and interdependence of disciplines and discrete areas of study within disciplines.

Collection development is responsive to instructional techniques, course goals and material publishing patterns in disciplines and occupational programs. Depth and breadth of collections are in part driven by student/faculty participation in resource-based teaching and learning.

Mindful of the community college's emphasis on educating and supporting the whole student, the library also purchases materials beyond the academic curriculum that relate to academic success, vocational guidance, and college transfer.

While philosophy is the most important criterion in the development of our collection, practical considerations such as budget and space constraints do impact decision making.

Initiating collections in response to new curriculum depletes resources available for existing instructional collections and programs. Such impacts should be carefully considered when developing new programs.

Materials not related to the curriculum that focus on personal, consumer, and/or recreational interests are minimally collected. More comprehensive collections in these areas are available through resource sharing and local public libraries.

C. General Selection Criteria

Selection is made on the basis of reviews[1]; recommendations by faculty, students and staff; current and retrospective bibliographies and lists of notable books; and other sources such as publishers' catalogs. Final selection decisions will be made by the Director of Library/Media Services and faculty librarians. Funds are not strictly allocated among the various academic divisions, although equity among programs is sought while giving consideration to the fact that cost of materials across disciplines is not equal.

Collection deficiencies receive priority in selection and are determined by considerations of collection use, course offerings, and collection balance.

---

[1] The Library faculty regularly selects from review sources such as: Booklist, Library Journal, New York Times Book Review, and School Library Journal, in addition to a variety of more specialized sources of reviews.

In order to provide for students' diverse reading levels, print materials with a range of readability levels are sought.

The collection includes some upper-division material for use by faculty and more advanced students.

The following criteria will be used for materials selection, as applicable:

- Materials shall support, and be consistent with, the general educational goals of the college and the objectives of specific courses.
- Materials shall meet high standards of quality in content and presentation.
- The most appropriate physical format will be selected, considering both the intended use and the cost.
- The selection of materials on controversial issues will be directed toward maintaining a balanced collection that represents various views. The entire range of human cultural practice and social expression is welcome in our collections. Once any library materials have been acquired, our concern is to make them available to as many patrons as may want them. Common sense and practical experience have indicated that theft and mutilation of socially sensitive library materials is common. For this reason, materials deemed to be at risk may be placed on Reserve, at the discretion of the library faculty.[2]
- Materials representing alternative points of view not embodied in mainstream literature will be sought.

D. Criteria for Specific Formats

1. Periodicals

Periodicals and newspapers are purchased or accepted as gifts for one or more of the following prioritized reasons:

- To keep the library's collections up-to-date with current information regarding the various subjects studied through Pierce College's instructional programs.
- To provide material not available in books and other media.
- To keep faculty and administration aware of recent developments in their fields.
- General reading.

Due to the expense of serials, and the commitment the college extends when adding a subscription, special attention will be given to coordination between campus libraries when selecting periodicals.

In addition to the general criteria for selection of all materials, individual titles are chosen and retained according to the following criteria:

- Relevancy of content to curriculum.
- Accessibility of content through indexes owned by Pierce College Libraries.
- Demand, as indicated by circulation statistics or requests.
- Representation of a subject or point of view needed in the collection.
- Cost of subscription in relation to potential use.
- Reputation of the periodical.

Periodicals will be acquired and retained in various formats - original paper, microfilm, microfiche, CD-ROM and online access. The format preferred for a specific title will be determined by careful consideration of the following criteria:

- availability
- space requirements
- ease of accessibility by students
- availability of equipment
- durability
- cost

Newspapers are purchased to give local, regional, national and international news coverage.

2. Periodical and Newspaper Back-files

Retention of periodical back-files will be considered on a title-by-title basis, and will depend on use statistics, potential reference value, and the availability of storage space. When storage space requires and cost allows, back-files will be retained in microfiche/film or CD-ROM format. (See #1 above for criteria.)

3. Computer Software

This format will be selected when it is the most appropriate format for the topic, the software presents a unique method of instruction, or the power of the computer permits manipulation of the information in a way that significantly enhances the information. Cost factors must be weighed against the educational and informational value of the software. IBM compatible format on 3½" disks is preferred, but others will be considered.

[2] Adapted from "The Selection and Treatment of Erotic or Other Controversial Materials in the University Libraries", Virginia Polytechnic Institute and State University, 1993.

Pierce College Library, Tacoma, Washington

4. Multiple Copies:

As a rule, the library does not purchase multiple copies of a title. Exceptions will be granted in such cases as when a work is assigned each quarter; or has high demand on both campuses; or is a "classic" in any given field, likely to get heavy use. Whenever possible, added copies shall be purchased in paperback editions.

When the library acquires a new edition of a previously-held title, the older editions shall be evaluated on an individual basis and retained, reclassified from reference to circulating, transferred to the other campus library, or withdrawn, as appropriate.

5. Videotapes/Laser Disks:

In addition to the standards set forth in "General Selection Criteria" (page 6), the following will be applied:

a. The material will be such that it can be best presented only in the video format. It will not, for example, be simply a recorded lecture, a series of still photographs, or material which could just as easily be published as a book unless it is the only format available.

b. It will be issued in a format (i.e. ½" VHS tape or 12" laser disk) for which playback equipment is readily available at Pierce College.

c. It should be offered at a price lower than the expected rental costs for the same item over a one-year period (taking into account not only the rental price but also the number of times the item would be rented on an annual basis).

6. Films:

In addition to the standards set forth in "General Selection Criteria" and in 5. c. above, the following will be applied:

a. Materials in the 16mm film format will be purchased only when they are not available as ½" VHS tapes or 12" videodisks, or when their special contents require the greater resolution capabilities and larger screen images of projected films.

7. Audio Tapes:

Cassette tapes shall be added to the collection when that format offers distinct advantages over print format, e.g., poetry read aloud by the poet; an interview with an author; foreign language instruction; music instruction. The library shall not, as a rule, purchase "Talking Book" versions of novels for listening rather than reading, except as appropriate in the New Reader collection.

8. Other:

Information in any format will always be considered for acquisition and will be judged by criteria such as relevance to curriculum or collection goals, cost, quality, and availability of equipment to operate or view it.

E. Special Collections

1. Reference Collection:

In addition to the standards set forth in "General Selection Criteria" (page 6), books will be selected for the reference collection with the intent of providing a comprehensive store of information on as wide a range of subjects as possible, including topics not represented in the general collection. Classification--placement of material within the reference collection--will be the responsibility of the Director of Library/Media Services and the faculty librarians.

Books will be housed in the Reference Collection for the following reasons:

a. Their organization and format are such that they are especially valuable as sources of ready information.

b. The demand for them is so great that they must be available in the library at all times.

c. They are so rare, expensive, or vulnerable to damage that they should not be circulated.

Books will be removed from the Reference Collection for the following reasons:

a. They have been superseded by newer, more up-to-date editions.

b. Their value as ready-reference sources has decreased to the point where they are no longer in constant demand, or they are no longer contributing to the overall comprehensive nature of the collection.

Books which have been removed from Reference but which still retain informational value may be reclassified for transfer to the general circulating collection or transferred between campuses.

2. Reserve Collection:

Library or personal materials may be placed in the limited-circulation Reserve Collection for a specific course or quarter at faculty request, provided that copyright regulations are adhered to. Other materials may be placed in the Reserve Collection due to monetary value, high use or risk of theft or damage. In all cases, faculty librarians make the final determination. As a general rule, Reference materials will not be placed on reserve.

3. Children's Literature Collection:

The Children's Literature Collection includes picture books for toddlers and preschoolers through age 5, and a representative selection of titles from the genre of children's literature that meet general curricular needs. It includes materials such as board books, song books, poetry, nonfiction or "concept" books, and fiction.

4. New Reader Collection:

This collection includes a variety of materials designed to meet the needs of newly literate adults and those learning English as a second language. Popular materials are collected at different levels of difficulty and are intended to encourage reading and foster language development. Although not a primary focus, some instructional materials and level-appropriate reference sources (e.g. dictionaries) are collected.

5. Maps:

The map collection includes political, thematic, and physical maps of all areas, as well as topographic maps of Washington state. Maps will be selected when their size, date, or topic is unique or superior to that provided in an atlas. Attention will be given to local maps not available in any other source.

6. Paperback Collection:

The library's Paperback Collection consists of donated books, primarily mass market paperbacks. This collection is intended to meet the recreational reading needs of students. These books are given minimal processing, are assigned no call numbers, and are not, as a rule, entered into INLEX. Exceptions are made when a title is in high demand or deemed of long term interest, in which case an added copy in the paperback collection will be noted in INLEX.

Books are never purchased for this collection; the only source is gifts. As a result, this collection is not balanced. At any given time it may emphasize science fiction, adventure or romance, depending on the nature of donations. Books are added to this collection when they are appropriate for the reading level and interest of the college community.

The paperback collection is understood to be less permanent than the cataloged collection, and books may be withdrawn and added frequently, due to the limited processing required.

7. Microforms:

In addition to back-files of periodicals (see sections V-D-1 and V-D-2), the library will maintain certain special collections in the microfiche or microfilm format (e.g. the <u>College Catalog Collection</u>). Consideration will be given to space, cost, access, durability, and the availability of a microfiche printer.

8. Slides/Filmstrips:

Materials in 35mm slide or filmstrip formats will be purchased only if the same or similar materials are not available in other formats <u>or</u> if the special content of these materials (such as art reproductions) requires the finer resolution capability, greater color fidelity and larger screen image of projected film.

9. Vertical File Materials:

Pamphlets shall be regularly selected and added to the vertical file in order to provide the most current information available on a wide variety of topics, with particular emphasis on local information and on those topics frequently chosen for student papers. In addition to pamphlets, photocopies of newspaper clippings of local interest may be added to the vertical file. Materials are selected at the discretion of the faculty librarian who oversees this collection. Pamphlets will be placed in this collection rather than other collections based on their ephemeral nature or physical characteristics.

Multiple copies of a pamphlet or clipping may be filed under several subject headings for ready access by students.

Because many vertical file materials quickly lose their usefulness, the vertical file shall be weeded more frequently than the permanent library collection.

F. Materials Not Selected

1. Textbooks:

Textbooks are not routinely purchased for the library collection, but are judged by the existing criteria for all materials. They are purchased when they are the most suitable format for supplementary reading, reference or research. Gifts of recent texts are accepted and added to the collection, if deemed potentially useful to students. The first preference will always be to purchase materials that complement required texts.

2. Materials Used In Class:

The library will not normally purchase lab manuals, textbooks students are expected to purchase, or reference material necessary for instruction. Nor will it collect books with formats unsuitable for multiple use, such as perforated tear-out pages or workbooks designed to be written in.

3. Serials Not Indexed:

As a rule, the library will not subscribe to periodicals not indexed in library-owned periodical indexes. However, when there are few indexed titles in a field (e.g. chemical dependency), exceptions will be made.

4. Graduate Level Research Materials:

Since the primary goal of the library is to meet the curricular needs of Pierce College students, the library will not collect upper-level materials or graduate-level materials to meet faculty research needs. Such needs will be met through interlibrary loan and referral to universities nearby.

5. Phonograph Records:

Phonograph records will not be purchased, that format having been effectively replaced by audio cassette tapes and compact disks.

G. Gifts

Gifts of books and other materials will be accepted under the following conditions:

1. All gift materials received by the Pierce College Library become the property of Pierce College. No materials received as gifts shall be returned to donors. If desired, the donors of gifts of exceptional value may be identified on mounted bookplates.

2. No special collections will be established except in accordance with the established collection design and development policy.

3. The Pierce College Library shall have the right to dispose of any gift materials which are not selected for addition to the library collection. Such disposition shall be in accordance with Washington State Law, and may include transfer to other libraries, sale, or discard. The Director of Library/Media Services or his/her designee shall make the final determination as to the disposition of all gift materials.

VI. COLLECTION MAINTENANCE

Systematic and regular withdrawal of materials from the collection benefits the Libraries by ensuring that the collections accurately reflect the current needs of the college communities. Selection and deselection are two aspects of the same continuous process of collection development and maintenance. Faculty librarians evaluate the collection periodically for library materials that have become obsolete, are physically unusable, or have low circulation. As part of their review, they will consult instructors with expertise in the relevant disciplines for advice concerning withdrawal of the material. The disposition of material shall be in accordance with Washington State Law.

Books and materials selected for removal must meet at least one of the following conditions before being discarded:

1. The material has been infrequently used for an extended period of time.

2. There is other material in the collection that fulfills the same need more adequately.

3. The physical condition of the material is such that it cannot be utilized, and repair would be impractical.

4. The age of the material is such that it is not useful for either current or historical purposes, or is no longer within the scope of the current collection development policy.

5. Duplicate copies of the title exist, and use does not mandate more than one copy.

Materials that are listed as sources in heavily-used indexes and bibliographies such as Play Index, Granger's Index to Poetry, etc., are retained unless physically unusable, and are then replaced, if possible. Titles from these sources that receive heavy use are checked in Books in Print before discarding, and are replaced with newer editions if available.

In examining the collection, faculty librarians reconsider each item in the light of the passage of time to determine whether or not it deserves a place on the shelf. The following categories will emerge:

1. Retain.

2. Withdraw: Subject matter out-of-date; no further issue potential; no longer consistent with curriculum.

3. Withdraw and Replace: Poor physical condition but the material is still useful; old edition to be replaced by a new edition.

After all reasonable efforts have been made to distribute withdrawn library materials, they will be offered for sale or discarded. The Director of Library/Media Services, or her/his designee, shall be the sole judge of the final disposition of discarded materials, in full compliance with Washington State Law.

PROCEDURE FOR REVIEW OF LIBRARY/MEDIA CENTER MATERIAL

Since free access to information is essential not only to education but to our democracy, the library upholds the principles of the American Library Association's "Freedom to Read" statement (Appendix B), and makes every effort to provide materials representing all points of view, including those which are unpopular or unorthodox. To quote directly from the Library Bill of Rights (Appendix A), "Censorship should be challenged by libraries in the maintenance of their responsibility to provide public information and enlightenment." This responsibility also entails establishing formal procedures for persons or groups wishing to request reconsideration of any material in the library collection.

Should a library user encounter material he or she feels is objectionable, the user has the right to complete a Statement of Concern Regarding Library Resources form (Appendix M). The form may be obtained at the reference desk or from the office of the Director of Library/Media Services, and the completed form must be submitted to the Director of Library/Media Services.

No material will be withdrawn, removed, or undergo a change in location or status until the entire review process is completed.

The patron's request will be received by the Director of Library/Media Services who will review the request with the faculty librarians and prepare a written response that includes an explanation for the decision to retain, withdraw or relocate the material in question. The explanation may include how the material relates to the educational goals of the college and the Library/Media Center, criteria used for selection of this and similar items, published reviews, and/or patron requests for and use of the material. Copies of the response will be submitted to the Executive Dean of Instruction.

Within three weeks of the postmark of the response from the Library/Media Center, the complainant may forward a written appeal to the Director of Library/Media Services. The Director will then, within two weeks of receipt of the appeal, establish and call the first meeting of an ad hoc Review Committee, whose members will be:

- two tenured faculty selected by the Faculty Association President (with at least one from the subject area of the material in question);
- one division chair (selected by the Executive Dean of Instruction);
- one library faculty member (selected by the Director of Library/Media Services) who is responsible for materials selection in the subject area of the material in question;
- one student (selected by Student Government);
- one librarian from the community (selected by the Director of Library/Media Services); and
- the Director of Library/Media Services.

The chair will be selected by the Committee.

The Committee will review the written request and the response, and will read, listen to, and/or view the material in question in its entirety. The library faculty member will provide information to the committee which may include:

- collection objectives that are met by the material;
- reviews from professionally recognized sources;
- statements by instructors whose students use or may use the material;
- any other information that could assist in defining the purpose or value of the material.

The Review Committee may rely on any resources of the college in arriving at a decision, taking into consideration the intellectual freedom documents of the American Library Association and Washington Library Association found in the appendices of this policy. The Committee may interview any other individuals, including the complainant, as well as seek counsel and advice from the Office of the Attorney General.

Within 45 days of receipt of the written appeal, the Committee will reach its decision with four or more concurring votes of the seven Committee members, and will forward the written decision and all documentation to the Director of Library/Media Services for action. The Director will notify the complainant in writing of the decision of the Committee and ensure the appropriate action has been complied with. Copies will be forwarded to the Executive Dean of Instruction.

Within two weeks of notification of the Committee's decision, the complainant or a dissenting member of the Committee may forward a written appeal to the President. Appeal decisions will be based on the material included in the file.

Material that has undergone a review may not be rechallenged for one calendar year from the date the Review Committee's recommendation is sent to the Director of Library/Media Services.

VIII. PERIODIC REVIEW

Since Pierce College is a dynamic institution, the Library's Collection Development and Materials Selection Policy must be responsive to change. Therefore, this policy will be reviewed periodically by the faculty librarians and the Library Faculty Advisory Committee, and revised accordingly.

IX. SAVING CLAUSE

Nothing contained in this policy shall conflict with the laws of the State of Washington or Pierce County, Washington, or with any policy established by Pierce College or the State Board for Community and Technical Colleges.

COLLEGE OF DUPAGE

Collection Devlopment Policies

I. ELEMENTS IMPORTANT TO COLLECTION DEVELOPMENT[1]

To say that the LRC is the heart of the college and that a college LRC is as good as the faculty it serves may sound trite, but these statements have a useful purpose. They identify the central importance of 1) the LRC in the college educational program, and 2) the faculty's role in the selection of materials for the LRC. In collection development, a plan for selection of materials is essential to build and maintain a collection that will best meet the curricular needs and community members' needs. Faculty involvement in selection, directed and coordinated by LRC staff among their various constituencies, is highly desirable if materials collection funds are to be spent more appropriately.

It is almost impossible to have a first-rate LRC collection that supports the curriculum offerings and community members' needs without a systematic, resourceful, and enlightened program of materials acquisition. There are some things which should be avoided and a few principles that should be recognized in developing a materials collection. Four aspects of collection development which must be given consideration are:

1. Size has little significance as a goal in building a materials collection. A plan of continuous discarding (weeding) is important, but it has the effect of keeping down the size of the collection. One reason that the number of volumes is too often emphasized in a collection is that it's easier to take a quantitative assessment than to make a qualitative appraisal of the collection.

2. It is necessary to recognize that the building of a first-rate collection is not an overnight project. When adding new courses to the curricula, consideration for supporting materials should be a first consideration. Once this is accomplished, along with day-by-day selection in response to the expressed needs of the faculty, students and staff, the need for a large "make-up" or "overtake" fund to fill in gaps will not be necessary. Quality collections come from a slow, consistent process of planned growth and development.

3. Recommended materials lists are suggestive, stimulating, and, when properly used, a helpful aid to selection. Excessive reliance upon these lists should be guarded against. Acquaintance with the materials themselves, critical reviews, and faculty recommendations are the best approaches to selection. A rigorous and systematic staff-faculty effort to materials selection can provide the desired collection as reflected by curricular and patron needs.

[1] Portions of this section are based on Guy R. Lyles's book, The President, the Professor, and the College Library. H.W. Wilson Company, 1963, pp. 34-50.

4. No single individual should be allowed to exercise undue control over LRC acquisitions. This would include any individual; the Dean, a division director, faculty or staff member. The LRC staff has a job of leadership but should exercise that role to coordinate and direct, and not to dominate materials selection.

A more positive approach to the development of building a materials collection is the realization that there must be a cooperative effort of administrators, faculty and LRC staff. Each has a role. The LRC staff's major concern is the development of the materials collection for which they assume the leadership role in building, and the Dean of LRC has ultimate responsibility for collection development through the implementation of a comprehensive collection development plan.

To promote administrtor, faculty, and LRC staff cooperation there are certain considerations which the LRC is compelled to study continuously and incorporate into its materials selection program. Among these are: 1) A clear understanding of what kinds of users; 2) an awareness of the different roles books and other materials play in filling basic informational needs and the intellectual life of those who come to the LRC; 3) an effective organization for involving the faculty and LRC staff in material selection; and 4) a liberal annual budget for materials acquisitions.

A. <u>Determining Type or Purpose of Collection</u>

The LRC staff (administrators and consultants) need certain information from the college's administrators and/or faculty to carry out their leadership role in materials collection building. The transplantation of that information within the framework of a collection development plan are critical in determining selection patterns and setting parameters. Answers are needed to such questions as: What is the anticipated student population? What is the maximum projection of the building capacity to house the collection? What disciplines (subjects) are currently being offered in the curricula? What changes are foreseen in the curricula over the next few years? Will the collection of materials be sufficient to meet the needs of the independent learner? Are materials available for the wide range of student capabilities? How does the non-student community user affect materials selection? These questions and others should be answered so a deliberate selection process can be used without selection under pressure of necessity. The LRC will be able to plan and control its collection growth far more usefully if the staff knows the goals and outcomes contemplated by the college's administration.

B. <u>Determining The Range of Resources To Be Included In The Collection</u>

The second consideration of successful materials collection building is the recognition by the administration and faculty that it takes different types of materials to fill different needs in curricular support and that each of these needs requires a rational and systematic program of materials selection. The types of resources to be considered are reference books, standard works, general works, and learning resources in other formats.

There are, for example, reference books that are needed for answering reference questions and for supplying background information. To assure that a good reference collection is available, proper provision for establishing and maintaining the collection to meet client needs is a rigourous, on-going process. Another group of materials essential to a good collection are the "standard" works. These materials include titles considered as being outstanding, including current materials in each subject area of the curriculum. These form the core of the heart of the collection. A third type of material is the often referred to "general works". These materials support, supplement, and give uniform coverage in the various subject areas that serve the college community, bridging the gap between the subjects taught and material of a general flavor. Other learning resources considered for selection (sometimes considered special collections) include pamphlet materials, periodicals, recordings (tape and phono), slides, 16mm films, filmstrips, videorecordings, microforms, and others which contribute to the infromation needs of the users. By naming certain types of materials that are needed to support the curriculum and general needs of LRC clientele, the enormity of materials selection becomes very clear and quite obviously a job demanding the cooperative efforts of many people.

C. Determining Organizational Structure For Collection Development

The third element in building the LRC collection which is important for administrators and faculty members to take into consideration is the need for effective organization. Without effective organization, materials selection can be haphazard, incomplete and superficial. Organization means that the LRC and faculty have formulated procedures for selecting and acquiring materials. It is organized so that the administration, faculty members and LRC staff recognize the importance of materials selection in the educational process and encourage widespread participation in doing a quality job. With adequate funding and organization, the Dean, faculty, and LRC staff can do their part.

1. The LRC's Administration Part (Dean and Directors)

Organizationally the Dean is concerned with the materials collection development program as a whole. The general responsibility for collection development is assigned by the Dean to the Directgor of Materials Utilization and Technical Services. Together, they see that policies and procedures for selecting and recommending various types of books and materials (reference works, standard works, general books, and other learning resources) are clearly defined and made known to those people in each curriculum area, small college department or division. They allocate the materials fund, making proper provision for each of the groups of materials fund, making the LRC collection. They provide for a two-way flow of information and ideas from the LRC to the faculty and from the Materials Utilization Consultants to the Dean and Director in the selection process. Because of his responsibility, the Dean has final authority for materials purchasing, including the right to disapprove materials orders which seem outside the LRC materials selection criteria.

2. The Faculty's Part

The faculty's responsibility in building the materials collection is essentially twofold. The first is keeping the collection up-to-date by thoughtful selection of new materials and weeding of the old. The second is to fill subject content gaps in the mateials collectin. A first step might be to make a survey of present LRC holdings in the subject area being evaluated. This could be accomplished by checking the LRC bibliographic data base against standard lists and selected titles compiled by the faculty from reviews appearing in professional journals and other materials selection aids. Each faculty member would be responsible for surveying needs in the field of his/her instructional area and be asked to list those materials considered essential for a good community college LRC.

To assist LRC staff in keeping the collection up-to-date or current, faculty members have a continuing responsibility to systematically check reviews in professional journals and other selection aids in his/her respective subject discipline. This is a responsibility faculty should cultivate as part of their contribution to collection development. Short of this the major portion of the collection development responsibility rests with the Materials Utilization Consultants to coordinate and expedite the evaluation/selection/collection development process.

Theoretically, the greater the participation of faculty in collection development, the heavier utilization of the materials collection by faculty and students will occur. This would be true because faculty would: 1) have a greater awareness of the materials in the existing collection; 2) recommend items for the collection they personally selected after evaluating the current collection; 3) be inclined to revise and incorporate LRC holdings in their course syllabus, and 4) encourage their students to utilize the LRC, knowing that a majority of their information needs could be serviced by the resources of the LRC. The greatest measure of a collection's strength is its relevance (usefulness) to the patron.

3. The LRC Staff's Part

Their chief contribution to developing the LRC collection is in the area of general and reference materials. The selecting of reference materials requires careful consideration so that monies expended for reference materials will be wisely spent. In the realm of general materials the LRC staff's efforts are directed to selecting materials that supplement, fill gaps and extend the selections made by faculty in their respective disciplines. Included here are the selection of fiction, poetry, essays, as well as general histories and history and criticism of literature, social histories, material on specific subject but treated in a genreal vain, biography and autobiography, description and travel, general science, general occupation/technical items, and so on.

D. Determining Budgetary Requirements For Collection Development

The last element to be considered here is the annual materials budget. Consideration must be given to several factors that affect the probable expenditure of materials funds in the LRC. These include the teaching methods in the college, price inflation of print and non-print materials, arrears in existing collections, and the materials evaluation/selection of its faculty. The latter factor is considered to be of a paramount importance for without it the LRC staff will find itself hard pressed to accurately reflect the curricular needs of the college's students and faculty.

In order to build a quality materials collection the previously mentioned four considerations are essential. To recapitulate, these were: 1) A clear understanding of the LRC program in relation to the total college program; 2) an awareness of the role various materials play in the informational needs and intellectual life of the patron; 3) being effectively organized so the faculty and LRC staff are cooperatively involved in materials selection; and 4) adequate funds to ensure a quality materials collection through wise selection of current publications and other learning resources. If the points mentioned in this document can be met by administrators, faculty and LRC staff thourgh a systematic, knowledgeable, and imaginative program of materials selection, then developing the materials collection that will meet the needs of the college community can be assured.

II. PURPOSE OF THE COLLECTION DEVELOPMENT MANUAL

1. Presents guidelines that may be used by the LRC staff, the college faculty and students in the building and development of the collection of materials for the LRC.

2. Support systematic and balanced building of the collection.

3. Provides a vehicle for the interpretaiton of selection policies and procedures to the students and faculty of the college.

4. Supports the concept of the interrelatedness of media in the collection.

5. Aids the staff in building a collection which reflects the philosophy, the educational program, the curriculum, the educational strategies employed by the College of DuPage.

6. Guarantees the proper transfer of internally produced materials from Media Services to Technical Services.

Since no collection development statements can be static, they must provide for meeting the overall goals and objectives of the Learning Resources Center which are as follows:

1. To coordinate programs and collections so that the LRC constantly reflects the purposes of the institution, the curriculum and educational program, and the instructional methods and techniques being used.

2. To promote the general cultural, recreational, vocational and career development of students, staff, faculty, and community members.

3. To promote the professional growth and development of the faculty.

4. To serve as a cultural center for community affairs.

5. To cooperate in community activities which can utilize the resources of the LRC.

6. To serve as the instructional hub of the college community.

7. To project itself outside the confines of any building restrictions so that it truly becomes the most vital instrument in the learning process.

With these broad goals in mind, these guidelines, policies and procedures must be flexible and ever-changing. In order to ensure that this flexibility is maintained, a standing committee composed of designated LRC personnel will meet once a year in May to consider any revision, deletions and additions.

III. RESPONSIBILITY FOR MATERIALS SELECTION

The general responsibility for materials selection is assigned by the Dean of LRC to the Director of Utilization and Technical Services. He supervises the selection process among the Utilization Consultants in his/her Division and among other LRC staff, faculty and students. The majority of the selection of materials will be done by:

1. The Utilization Consultants generating selection by working with faculty in the individual Divisions and within his/her assigned subject areas following the guidelines of the Intensive Evaluation Selection Plan.[1] This will include, a) individual faculty requests, b) requests for basic collections for new programs, c) requests for basic collections for individual courses. See Appendix A for Utilization Consultants' discipline assignments.

2. The Utilization Consultants selecting from current standard lists, guides, reviews, etc.

3. The Utilization Consultants selecting from standard bibliographies in specific subject areas or bibliographies of materials for community college and academic libraries.

The reviewing and previewing of all materials will be a regular function of the professional staff of the Division. All professional staff will participate in the selection process. This is not a function of exempt or classified personnel. Realizing that the selection of materials is only one of multiple responsibilities of the area of Utilization, no single staff member can be assigned this sole responsibility.

Utilization Consultants that have special format collection responsibility, such as pamphlets, periodicals, reference, non-print items, are ultimately responsible for a balanced, current collection of materials to these formats which span all subject areas. It is possible for all LRC consultants, faculty, and other people to recommend items in these special collections with the final judgment made by the special format collection consultant.

Each Utilization Consultant is responsible for selecting materials which serve the educational program of the college and involve college faculty in the materials selection process. Specific responsibilities are:

1. Reviewing, previewing and selecting materials in all media formats in specific subject areas assigned which are appropriate to the college's educational and service program.

2. Coordinating and directing faculty and staff in an in-depth analysis of specific subject areas according to the Collection Development Schedule by Discipline (See Appendix B).

3. Coordinating and approving the acquisition of certain materials in specific subject areas and materials formats.

a. Special collection requests (pamphlets, periodicals, reference works) are forwarded to the Utilization Consultant responsible for the maintenance and development of the particular format.

4. Examining circulation statistics to determine the utilization of the materials in subject areas.

5. Assisting Technical Services personnel in searching for hard-to-find materials, out-of-print materials and other problems areas in the ordering process.

6. Giving assistance to Technical Services personnel in the processing of locally-produced materials.

7. Cooperate with the other Utilization Consultants in recommending titles for those special collections; e.g., pamphlets, periodicals, and reference items, in the subject areas assigned.

8. Recommending to the Director of Utilization and Technical Services those materials needing discarding in the subject areas of responsibility.

9. Responding to school, state, and national reports on the resources of the subject areas in the LRC collection.

General Process:

1. All orders generated internally or externally will be routed to the Utilization Consultant responsible for selection in the subject area of request.

2. He/she will pull out what he/she considers to be "problem" requests. These may be identified on the basis of excessive cost, duplication of copies of type of material already in the LRC, multiple copies, lack of proper identification of item, etc.

3. The remaining requests (exceptions noted in #5 and 6 below) will be turned over to the appropriate Acquisitions Assistant for immediate ordering.

4. Those "problem" requests remaining will be referred to and discussed with the Director of Utilization and Technical Services. Order cards will be returned by the Director of Utilization and Technical Services (or the Utilization Consultant) to the originator of the order for the following reasons: a) the budgetary situation, b) the need for multiple copies of a single item, and c) similar items already in the collection. Requests which cannot be resolved otherwise should be referred to the Dean of Learning Resources.

5. Non-print items costing above $100 must be ordered in for preview and evaluated by the appropriate subject Utilization Consultant and faculty member(s). Recommendations are routed to the Non-Print Order Assistant.

6. Non-print items costing more than $100 must have consensus through written recommendations by those previewers listed above in #5. See Section VII - Preview and Purchas Policies and Procedures For Non-Print Materials of this manual for details.

7. All staff at all times should feel that they have the freedom and the responsibility to advise the Director of Materials Utilization and Technical Services about individual concerns that they might have regarding specific items being considered for purchase.

IV. INTENSIVE EVALUATION/SELECTION PLAN

A. Purpose:

The purpose of the Intensive Evaluation/Selection plan is to systematically and periodically evaluate the materials collection, selecting appropriate materials that will contribute to strengthening the college's educational program and resources for community members. The plan ensures an on-going program of collection development and maintenance that provides direction for comprehensive, long-range planning the LRC's materials collection.

B. Inventory Schedule For Collection Development

Each Utilization Consultant develops a five-to-seven-year collection program/discipline development schedule for intensive evaluation in his/her assigned areas. (See Appendix B). The nature of each subject area determines how often it should be intensively appraised. In areas where information quickly becomes obsolete, such as science and technology, appraisal is done more often than in more stable areas such as literature and history.

C. Policies and Procedures

1. During Fall Quarter, each Utilization Consultant prepares a written plan of implementation for the area(s) to be intensively evaluated for that academic year. The plan is submitted to the Dean of LRC and the Director of Utilization and Technical Services for approval. The approved plan is shared with other Materials Utilization Consultant(s) whose areas of selection are involved. The plan includes:

   a. Courses offered and the names of faculty teaching those courses in the specific subject area(s) being evaluated.

   b. Library of Congress classifications which match subject area(s). Classifications which are not part of the college curriculum are included. (See Appendix C).

   c. Number of items being evaluated.

   d. Approach to faculty participation, i.e. one-to-one meeting, invitation to all faculty in discipline, large group meeting followed by small group meetings, other approaches.

   e. Titles of bibliographic and selection aids to be used by faculty and Utilization Consultant(s).

   f. A sample copy of the memo(s) to be sent to faculty including statement of purpose, meeting dates, topics to be discussed at initial meeting(s), and tentative completion date for the entire process.

D. Implementation:

Implementation of the Intensive Evaluation/Selection Plan is based on the plan approved by the Dean of the LRC and the Director of Utilization and Technical Services. Specific policies and procedures are:

1. Memos are sent to appropriate faculty.

2. Packets of materials are prepared for initial meetings with faculty. These packets contain statistical computer printouts, a list of periodicals, current bibliographies, a list of selection aids, order cards and the Collection Development Questionnaire (Appendix D).

3. Selection and weeding criteria are explained to faculty. (The Collection Development Manual may be shared with faculty.)

4. Requests for materials are handled in the same manner as day-to-day requests.

5. Faculty are requested to designate those items in the statistical computer printouts which they feel should be weeded.

6. Other Utilization Consultants whose areas of selection are involved in the process may attend the initial meetings, and will be consulted before items in their selection areas are purchased or discarded.

7. Participating faculty are asked to complete the Complete Development Questionnaire and return it to the Utilization Consultant. Decisions on faculty requests for materials to be added to the collection or weeded from the collection are subject to the professional judgment of the Utilization Consultants, and the Director of Utilization and Technical Services.

When there is little or no cooperation on the part of the faculty, the sole responsibility for implementation of the Intensive Evaluation/Selection process rests with the Utilization Consultants.

E. Documentation:

At the conclusion of the collection development process for each area, a summary of activities and an evaluation of the collection area assessed is submitted, to the Dean of the LRC and the Director of Utilization and Technical Services, along with the completed Collection Development Questionnaires from participating faculty.

The summary discusses faculty participation, strengths and weaknesses of the assessed area, selection and weeding activities.

The documentation may also be shared with other Utilization Consultants.

V. CRITERIA FOR MATERIALS SELECTION

A. Print Materials

1. Books

To be consistent with the philosphy of the College of DuPage, the LRC book collection must reflect the needs not only of faculty and students but the community at large. Community needs will be served through cooperative efforts involving the public libraries, the public library system and other colleges in the community. In serving faculty and students, the major criterion is the relevance of the material to the educational aims and purposes of the institution. Factors to be considered are demands of curriculum, interests of faculty and students, subject area weaknesses, and enrollment trends.

Specific criteria for selection of individual titles are:

Anticipated use
Accuracy
Authority
Scope
Literary merit
Level of treatment
Format
Timeliness of publication
Cost

Critical reviews from reputable book selection tools are used as well as first-hand evaluation whenever possible.

Cost is weighed against the title's overall usefulness to the strength of the collection in that subject area.

Requests for highly specialized materials for individual faculty and student use will be handled through the services of inter-library loan and microforms.

Textbooks will be purchased only when the work is definitive or other special features make it worthwhile addition to the collection.

Paperback books will be purchased only when no hardbound edition of the title is available. In this case the book will be bound before being added to the collection unless the publication is a serial which will be superseded in the near future (e.g. Consumer Reports Annual Buying Guide). These will ordinarily be kept in the Reference Collection. (Revise in 1985-86)

2. Pamphlets

The primary function of the pamphlet collection is to provide up-to-date material. Selection of pamphlets follows the general policies outlined for book selection with the following exceptions:

Because of the ephemeral nature of the material, less attention need be paid to format and lasting worth to the collection.

Since pamphlet material is normally free or inexpensive, multiple copies may be obtained as need arises.

Any pamphlet may be cataloged if access through the computer catalog seems desirable.

3. <u>Periodicals</u>

   a. Any member of the college staff, faculty, student body or community may request that a title be added to the collection.

   b. When a new title is requested, the LRC orders a complementary copy from the publisher in order to evaluate it.

   c. A periodical title is evaluated in terms of the same criteria given for books but with the following special emphasis:

      i. Does the title reflect sourse needs:
      ii. Does the title's projected degree of usage justify its cost?
      iii. If not, does the LRC have quick access to the title through inter-library loan?
      iv. Is the content of the title duplicated in other titles which the LRC carries?
      v. Are the titles' contents readily accessible by means of an index?
      vi. Is the content able to be understood by a broad segment of the student body?
      vii. Does the title satisfy popular interest?

   d. The entire periodical collection will be continuously evaluated in terms of the above criteria and in accordance with the Collection Development Schedule. New titles recommended for purchase or titles recommended for deletion should be submitted to the Utilization Consultant responsible for coordinating periodical collection development. New title arrival notification will be according to current procedures.

   e. A title which contains material of permanent reference value, validity for course or reference needs and is likely to have a high degree of usage will be retained permanently, either on microfilm or bound, unless the title is not indexed by any indexing service. Titles will be retained on microfilm unless the value of the illustrations would be lost in black and white microfilm format. Current issues of a title will be discarded as soon as they are replaced by microfilm. Titles which are not retained in bound or microfilm format will be discarded in most cases after three calendar years; e.g., in January, 1986, all of the 1982 issues would be discarded. Exceptions to the three year discard policy will be designated by the Utilization Consultant responsible for periodicals.

f. Discarded issues will be disposed of as follows:

i. Discarded issues for which the LRC may areceive credit will be shipped to a dealer in back-issues or periodicals;
ii. Discarded issues will be exchanged with other libraries able to supply the LRC with issues wanted for binding;
iii. Discarded issues remaining will be listed in The Bulletin as available on a first come, first served basis;
iv. All issues remaining will be made available to any interested person.

B. Non-print Material

The emphasis on the utilization of non-print materials in instructional programs requires a continuous organized non-print materials selection program.

Careful evaluation on non-print material is essential when considering acquisition of the material. Because of the expense of non-print materials, every effort should be made to assure the acquisition of the best material available in the area of need. The capabilities of Media Production should be considered when selecting commercially-prepared materials. The producer's annotation should not be used solely as a selection aid when making the decision to purchase. Some guidelines of the evaluation process are:

1. Use of systematic approach in the selection process. Avoid the waste of duplicating appraisals of materials or applying different sets of criteria, with the result that appraisals cannot be compared or evaluated. Record the resulting data for future use.

2. When possible view several titles on the topic desired before purchasing.

3. Include faculty and students in evaluating whenever possible. Subject experts can best point out weaknesses and strengths in the content.

In the selection of non-print materials the general factors and criteria that apply to print materials are relevant (See Section A). The selection of non-print materials is based on criteria relating to the characteristics of all types of non-print materials. These criteria may be stated as:

1. The material should be technically satisfactory (with respect to sound, type size, photography, narrative style, color, etc.).

2. Consideration of the material's cost and the time and effort required to use it should be weighted against some less expensive materials that may produce equal or even better results.

3. Consider the various formats and select the one that treats the topic in the best manner. The type of use (group or individual) should be a factor.

   Materials produced in Media Production and student-produced materials will be added to the collection if the material meets the criteria stated for that type of media.

For a list of criteria type questions when evaluating and selecting various types of non-print materials, see Appendix M.

VI. PROCEDURES FOR HANDLING REQUESTS AND PROCESSING LOCALLY-PRODUCED MATERIALS THAT ENHANCE THE LRC MATERIALS COLLECTION

1. When a request is made for Media Production services, the Production staff will check to see if material on the subject has previously been produced and is available in the Master Production File. The Utilization Consultant responsible for selection in the subject area, when requested by Production staff, will check the materials catalog to determine if material on the subject is available in the LRC materials collection.

2. If the requested material is not available in the LRC collection, but is available commercially it should be determined by the Utilization Consultant responsible for selection in the subject area whether the material should be ordered for preview from a commercial source.

3. If it is determined that suitable material is not in the LRC collection nor available from a commercial source, then work may be initiated for local production of the material.

4. After Production work is completed the Director of Media Production has the material routed to the Utilization Consultant. The decision on including it in the LRC materials collection will be made by the Utilization Consultant responsible for selection in the subject area and the Director of Media Production before the patron is notified of the materials availability. (See Section V.B. for general and specific criteria.)

5. If it is decided to include the material in the LRC collection, the material will be routed to Technical Services for immediate cataloging and processing. A synopsis either written by the instructor or Production personnel, will accompany the material to assist in cataloging the item. Information will include whether it is color, black and white, length in minutes, course name and number, and the instructor's name.

6. As soon as the material has been cataloged Technical Services will notify the original requestor of the material's availability for check-out.

7. All locally produced materials designated through this process as worthy of adding to the collection will have a protection copy retained in a master file in the appropriate Production area.

8. During the collection development process, carried out by the Utilization area, referrals may be made by Utilization personnel when material about a particular topic is needed to enhance the collection and suitable material is not available commercially.

VII. PREVIEW AND PURCHASE POLICIES AND PROCEDURES FOR NON-PRINT MATERIALS

Requests for preview and possible purchase of non-print materials may originate from faculty, LRC staff, administrative staff and include the following:

1. The originator of a non-print preview request may submit the request to the Non-Print Order Assistant or his/her LRC Utilization Consultant assigned to the Division or administrator unit.

2. The LRC holdings are checked and if the item is not in the collection the request for preview is forwarded to the Non-Print Order Assistant. (Preview is not mandatory for non-print items costing $100 or less.)

3. When the preview item arrives, the orginator(s) of the request and the appropriate Utilization Consultant are notified by the Audiovisual Clerks. Utilization Consultants may suggest other names of college staff who may be interested in the subject of the non-print item.

4. Preview of the item is arranged through the Audiovisual Clerks. The Utilization Consultant previews the item. Faculty and other interested staff may choose to preview the item with their Utilization Consultant as well as with colleagues in a group-viewing session.

5. "Non-Print Materials Evaluation Forms" are supplied and evaluators are expected to complete the forms which serve as a guide for possible purchase. (See Appendix E).

6. See Appendix F for details on routing and approval of non-print items.

7. If the Utilization Consultant decides to recommend the item for purchase, a "Rationale for Purchase of Non-Print Materials" form is completed by the Utilization Consultant and returned to the Non-Print Order Assistant. These forms will be retained for two years.

8. Both copies of the "Rationale for Purchase of Non-Print Materials" form and a requisition are submitted to the Director of Utilization and Technical Services.

9. When the Director of Utilization and Technical Services approves the Item, the "Rationale for Purchase of Non-Print Materials" forms are submitted to the Dean of LRC for approval.

    a. If the Director of Utilization and Technical Services does not recommend pruchase of the item, he/she returns the "Rationale for Purchase of Non-Print Materials" forms with the reason(s) for non-recommendation to the Utilization Consultant requesting the item.

10. If the item is approved for purchase by the Dean the appropriate paper work is routed back to the Non-Print Order Assistant for final action.

    a. If an item is not approved for purchase by the Dean, he/she returns both copies of the form to the Utilization Consultant with reason(s) for non-recommendation.

11. When the purchase ordering process is completed, the Non-Print Order Assistant files the white copy of the rationale form in the appropriate file.

12. Utilization Consultants and faculty that previewed items are notified by the Non-Print Order Assistant when the item has been purchased. See Appendix G-1.

VIII. PURCHASE OF RENTAL NON-PRINT MATERIALS

When a non-print item is requested frequently for rental, the decision may be made to purchase the item. The decision to purchase non-print materials which are requested for rental will be based upon the following considerations:

1. Consideration will be given to the demand for utilization by instructors whether the title will be ordered for classroom and/or student assigned viewing several times each year or only on one or two occasions.

2. Consideration will be given to the nature of the film or video subject matter and treatment whether it is of highly specialized character or if it be of limited contemporary interest (i.e. containing potentially "dated" or "dating" material).

3. Consideration will be given to the low-rental availability, ease or difficulty of access when requested - and cost factors involved (i.e. if it is only available from high rental sources; if it can be purchased without unreasonable costs involved, etc.).

IX. MULTIPLE COPIES OF MATERIALS

The LRC will buy one copy of each title approved for purchase.

The LRC will acknowledge all faculty requests for quantity purchases of single items, either book or non-print, of up to three copies if use and demand warrant. Any request for more than three copies of a single item will be evaluated on an individual basis by the Director of Utilization and Technical Services and the appropriate Utilization Consultants.

Requests for additional copies must be justified, taking into consideration: 1) past demand, 2) existing materals in the collection, and 3) specific or unique needs that justify the purchase of more than three copies of the same title.

X. FACULTY MATERIALS REQUESTS FOR PERSONAL USE IN OFFICES

The LRC does not purchase books, periodicals or other materials intended for personal use in faculty offices. These requests may be directed by faculty members to the division deans.

XI. GIFTS

Policies:

Gift materials accepted by the LRC are added to the collection only if they meet the criteria used for purchase of materials (See Section V of the "Collection Development Manual"). Since there is great cost in processing all materials, new and gift, the Materials Utilization Consultants must exercise caution in adding gifts instead of selecting new materials. In addition to the list of criteria for purchasing new materials, the following guidelines exist to assist the Consultants in the disposition of gift materials:

1. Physical condition and anticipated use are primary criteria.
2. Textbook and paperback books are added if they meet the criteria for purchase of materials.
3. Duplicates are not added, except when high circulation figures, a history of replacement, or demonstrated heavy use indicates a need for an additional copy.

The Gift Materials Utilization Consultant will inform all donors before the gift materials are accepted of the LRC's right to determine their retention, location, cataloging treatment, and other considerations related to their use or disposition. No special collection will be set up and maintained as a unit within the LRC.

Large donations will be picked up at the donor's location if so requested.

Periodical donations are referred to the Utilization Consultant in charge of periodicals for approval.

The Gift Materials Utilization Consultant will refer those significant gift items which should be acknowledged by the Board of Trustees to the Dean of Learning Resources. Monetary gifts to purchase materials are turned over to the Director of Utilization and Technical Services for deposit in the proper account. Materials given in memoriam will be given nameplates if so requested.

No value appraisals will be written for the donor by the LRC. A letter acknowledging the acceptance of the gift will be sent to the donor by the Gift Materials Utilization Consultant in which space is made for the donor to insert an appraisal figure.

Procedures:

1. The Gift Materials Utilization Consultant will receive telephone calls or make personal contact with the prospective donor. Every effort will be made at this point to determine their value for the LRC. The Consultant may refer the donor to other agencies that may accept their gifts, e.g. DuPage Library System, area book exchanges and book sales.

2. Upon receipt of the donations the Gift Materials Utilization Consultant will discard items that definitely do not meet the criteria cited above.

3. The Gift Materials Utilization Consultant will arrange the remainder into broad subject categories and then give them to the Acquisitions Senior Library Aide who will check the LRC holdings for duplicates, other editions, and circulation statistics.

4. The Acquisitions Senior Library Aide will place the items on a book truck for the Materials Utilization Consultants consulting in the pertinent subject areas to review and determine the final disposition of the items.

5. The Acquisition Senior Library Aide will prepare a gift letter to the donor signed by the Gift Materials Utilization Consultant. See Appendix H for sample letter.

XII. <u>REPLACEMENT OF LOST AND DAMAGED MATERIAL</u>

For lost or damaged material the same general and specific criteria for selection will apply in determining if the material is to be replaced in the LRC collection.

Additional Criteria for Replacement of Lost or Damaged Materials Includes:

1. Copyright date. Is there more recent materials?

2. Past usage. Number of times checked out, but also noting length of time materal was in the collection.

3. Other material in collection covering the subject.

4. If decision is made reorder, are additional copies needed?

This decision to replace lost and/or damaged print materials will be made by the Utilization Consultant in charge of that particular subject area.

XIII. STANDING ORDERS

Standing orders for monographic series will be placed only after examination of at least one title in the series and the list of published titles (when available).

Annual publications (almanacs, yearbooks, etc.) needed in the collection should be obtained on a standing order basis to insure up-to-date information. This is especially true of material in the reference collection.

Decisions on standing order selections rest with the Utilization Consultant responsible for that particular subject area and/or special collection. Decisions on standing orders for the reference collection is the responsibility of the Utilization Consultant coordinating the maintenance of the reference collection.

XIV. SPECIAL COLLECTIONS

Special collections are defined as materials that have been selected by faculty and LRC personnel, purchased with college funds, cataloged and processed for the constituencies of the college community. They are either housed in the LRC or external to the LRC and identified physically as separate, distinct special purpose collections.

Examples of internal special collections are Planning Information Center for Students (PICS) and the juvenile collection. An effort will be made as far as budget and space allowed to collect all available materials on the geographic area served by the College of DuPage.

A. Internal Special Collections - Characteristics of and guidelines for the development of internal LRC special collections.

1. JUVENILE COLLECTION

   a. The juvenile collection shall be restricted to materials generally considered appropriated for children and juveniles, twelve (12) years of age and under.

   b. All print and non-print materials which are identified by appropriate LRC staff or faculty as juvenile materials and which meet the goals listed in the policy statement for the juvenile collection will be placed in a special collection apart from the regular circulating LRC collection.

   c. All materials designated for this collection will be cataloged using the LC Classification system and shelved accordingly within the special collection.

d. All item records will indicate the shelf location "Juvenile" in order to inform the patrons that the material is part of that special collection.

e. The purpose, goals, and intended audience are detailed in "Juvenile Collection", Appendix I.

2. PLANNING INFORMATION CENTER FOR STUDENTS (PICS)

Until such time as the Master Plan for PICS is implemented, the Planning Information Center for Students will remain a collection of materials intended for use within the Center. Materials will be selected and arranged to facilitate browsing, self-exploration and planning of educational opportunities, various occupations, careers in the U.S. Armed Forces and the employment search process. Materials necessary to support the PICS concept will be selected in a variety of print and audiovisual formats in accordance with the criteria established in this manual.

To fulfill its defined purpose, the PICS collection will include some titles found in the LRC Reference Collection. This duplication will include directories of 2-year, 4-year, occupation/technical and "alternative" schools as well as The Occupational Outlook Handbook, The Directory of Overseas Summer Jobs - and similar items.

Some materials selected for PICS may also warrant use by an individual for prolonged study. For any items so identified, an additional copy will be ordered for the LRC circulating collection. Examples might include the series, Your Future in..., books on how to write a resume or test preparation materials (CLEP, GED, SAT, etc.)

Being a special purpose collection, many of the items in PICS will be housed exclusively in the Center. The detailed information on careers and individual colleges is typical of items found only on PICS. More specifically PICS will house the Career Monographs Series; the SRA Career Pamphlet File; current issues of journals on careers and the world of work; the Catalyst booklets; the set of Talking Transfer tape; microfiche collection of college catalogs, college information (catalogs, brochures, application forms); brochures and filmstrips on military careers; current C/D program brochures, Job Opportunity Bulletin, Advisor's Handbook and other C/D publications and numerous other book and audiovisual items and pamphlet materials.

All materials will be cataloged by the LC Classification system and the identifier "PICS" located on the label above the call number. All item records for material only available in PICS will be given the designation PICS in order to inform the patron that the material is part of that special collection.

3. RENTAL VIDEOCASSETTE PROGRAM IN LRC

Background:

Late in 1980 and early in 1981 the LRC staff studied the feasibility of providing rental videocassettes for check out by students, faculty, staff and community borrowers. It was determined that such a program would be beneficial to the LRC's program of services and that this program would probably pay for itself.

On April 18, 1981, the Board of Trustees passed an agenda item to purchase a basic collecton of videocassettes. The selection of videocassettes had already been made by the library staff. So purchase, cataloging and processing of this collection took place in late April and early May. Circulation of the videocassettes began in early May, 1981.

Policies and Procedures:

The rental fee is still $2.50 for 3-days for students and community borrowers, and $1.00 for 3-days for college faculty and staff. A collection of older tapes is available to all for $1.00 for a 3-day period. Other policies and procedures are constantly being evaluated to insure continued success of the program. These include fee structure, copyright protection, inspection, marketing, cleaning length of check-out, and evaluation of content of new tapes being purchased to insure suitability for our collection. In 1983-84 Subject and Title lists were made available to patrons to insure ease of access to the collection. In 1984-85 a brochure was developed for public relations purposes.

B. External Special Collections

External special collections are those college authorized instructional program laboratories, e.g., the Nursing Lab and Skills Center.

External LRC collections will be governed in accordance with the following statement:

> "All college services offered by the LRC and Skills Center remain centralized with the option to decentralize facilties and resources into small resource labs as individual college needs demand." Quote from College of DuPage "Model for Reorganization", page 13, dated January 15, 1971.

The policy statement and guidelines for the development and maintenance of external LRC special collections housed in college authorized instructional program labs follows.

1. Instructional Program Labs

Policy: The LRC will purchase and process materials for instructional program laboratories according to the guidelines enumerated below.

The following guidelines provide a framework for inclusions of materials in designated program labs:

1. Items appearing on course syllabus that are essential to students' study activities in the lab will be housed in a lab as long as they continue to be on the course syllabus. These items should be designated (by an asterisk) on the syllabus by the instructor teaching the course. Any exception to the above must be authorized by the director or coordinator of the program and the Director of Utilization and Technical Services. Multiple copies can be added to a lab (depending on anticipated needs and use) when authorized by the director of coordinator of the program and the Director of Utilization and Technical Services.

2. Basic ready-reference materials, such as dictionaries and handbooks, that will aid students in understanding terminology, procedures, etc. can be added to lab on a permanent basis.

3. All items that are requested for lab use (as in 1 and 2 above) must be authorized by the director or coordinator of the program and purchase approval given by the Director of Utilization and Technical Services.

4. Materials no longer needed for a particular course are to be returned to the LRC (Director of Utilization and Technical Services) with a recommendation to place in the collection for circulation or discard due to obsolescense, etc.

5. All materials purchased will be cataloged and processed before distribution to labs.

For policies and procedures on faculty requests for modules of instructional and/or complete courses, see the General Policies and Procedures Manual.

The following guidelines can be used to determine materials that will be housed in and circulated from the LRC:

1. Items not essential to students' study activities in the labs but appearing on the syllabus as supplemental materials are housed in and circulated from the LRC. These items need not be authorized by the Director or coordinator of the program, but will be approved by the LRC subject specialist in accordance with the <u>Collecton Development Manual</u>.

2. Short supplemental readings appearing on course syllabus (those that require 15 minutes or longer of reading) can be placed on reserve at circulation desk and designated for "Room Use Only" in the LRC.

3. Multiple copies, in addition to those ordered specifically for the lab, can be requested for the LRC collection at the discretion of the program coordinator and/or the LRC subject specialist.

None of the above precludes faculty from requesting materials for the circulating collection of the LRC, which supports the programs direct instruction or may be of related interest to the patrons of the LRC.

XV. WEEDING CRITERIA

Circulating Collection:

General considerations for discarding materials are:

Circulation statistics
Last date of circulation
Timeliness
Reliability
Ephemera
Physical condition
Duplicates

Items usually not discarded are those which have research value, are out-of-print, cover local history, and add balance to the collection.

Reference Collection:

Books replaced by newer editions, more complete versions, or more authoritative titles will be discarded or added to the circulating collection if of sufficient value. See Section VI-C of the Reference Collection Policy for further detail.

XVI. CENSORSHIP

The LRC does not promote particular beliefs or views. It serves the individual with resources so he can examine issues freely and make his own decisions. We therefore reaffirm the statement of the Library Bill of Rights of the American Library Association (Appendix J).

Those subjects which are frequent topics of criticism are considered below:

Religion - Factual unbiased material which represents religious views should be included in the LRC collection or be made available to the patron through other sources. Ideologies - The LRC should, without making any effort to sway reader judgment, make available factual information on the level of its reading public, on any ideology or philosophy which exerts a strong force, either favorable or unfavorable in government, current events, politics, education, or any phase of life which might be of interest to patrons.

Sex and Profanity - Sexual incidents or profanity should not automatically disqualify material. The decision should be made on the basis of whether the material presents life, whether the circumstances are realistically dealt with, and whether the material is of literacy value. Factual material of an education nature on the level of the reader should be included in the LRC collection.

Science - Medical and scientific knowledge should be made available without biased selection of facts.

Procedures for Handling Complaints:

Persons objecting to the suitability of particular books or other materials in the Learning Resources Center are referred to the Dean of the Learning Resources Center. If no resolution of the complaint is reached, the Dean of the Learning Resources Center will offer other alternatives to the complaint. (See Appendix K).

XVII. INTERLIBRARY COOPERATION

The College of DuPage is located in an area which contains many libraries of various types and several cooperative ventures involving these libraries. It is imperative that we utilize these to the fullest in order that we may spend our own budget most wisely and offer the fullest service to all citizens of our district. Interlibrary loan arrangements with the public library systems, the local colleges, and the State Library is utilized as fully as possible, especially for those materials which are too specialized for inclusion in our collection or out-of-print materials. OCLC, a national online bibliographic database, also enables the LRC to borrow materials from libraries across the United States.

In return, we must be as generous as possible in our procedures in loaning materials to citizens through these agencies. It is highly desirable to work through these channels to avoid unnecessary loans and ensure proper responsibility for the material.

For specific policies and procedures on interlibrary see the General Policies and Procedures Manual.

Houston Community College System

2.0 Public Services
2.3 Collection Development

.1 Collection Development

.1.1 Introduction

The acquisition and maintenance of the library's materials collection is a primary function of the library's mission in support of the College's objectives.

Collection development refers to the process of building and maintaining the library's entire materials collection, in both print and non-print formats. The collection development process includes the formulation of policy and procedure, coordination of activities, budget formulation and allocation, needs assessment, collection evaluation, selection, resource sharing and weeding.

.1.2 Responsibility for Collection Development

The ultimate responsibility for the development of the library's materials collection rests with the Director of Libraries/Learning Resources.

Under the policies, procedures and guidelines approved by the director, the Coordinator of Public Services is responsible for the overall growth and development of the collections.

Within the framework of Public Services each fulltime librarian is assigned system-wide responsibility for collection development and materials selection in particular subject areas.

.1.3 Goals

.1.3.1 Collection development is an ongoing activity designed to meet the following goals through the selection and acquisition of materials:

To provide a broad spectrum of materials representing a balance of points of view, in a variety of formats, in support of the instructional needs of the student body, faculty, and staff.

2.0 Public Services
2.3 Collection Development

To establish and maintain policies and procedures that encourage a broad range of participation in the collection development process, involving both the library as well as faculty, staff and students throughout the college.

To provide guidelines for the systematic development and evaluation of the collection.

To provide interdependent campus library collections that address needs of each specific campus as well as the overall needs of the system.

To maintain an awareness of the library and college's role in the community and to be aware of those community needs that may have an effect on the library.

To develop an informed appreciation of other local or regional resources available to faculty and students, as a supplement to the library's resources.

.1.4 Priorities

.1.4.1 The primary function of the library collection is to provide materials that support the educational process. This is accomplished in two interrelated ways:

Support to students through the provision of course-related and research materials.

Support to faculty through the provision of materials for use in classroom instruction.

.1.4.2 Secondarily, the library provides some materials designed to support the following areas:

Local and state information

Curriculum development and effective classroom techniques

Materials on the state of community colleges

.1.4.3 Finally, materials supporting cultural and recreational interests, and materials that foster personal growth and awareness are purchased in limited quantities, depending on funds, interest and space.

.1.4.4 The library is not able to purchase materials for individual faculty research projects.

.1.5 Activities Involved

.1.5.1 The Coordinator of Public Services has the responsibility for developing and implementing policies and procedures to achieve collection development goals:

For providing annual budgetary input for materials acquisitions and equitable distribution of the materials budget among the subject specialists.

For utilizing the knowledge and talents of the subject specialists effectively.

For providing review of day-to-day selection as needed.

For promoting full participation in the collection development process by all library staff.

For promoting full participation of all college faculty and students in the collection development process.

.1.5.2 Fulltime librarians, acting as subject specialists, have the primary responsibility for system-wide collection development and day-to-day materials selection and weeding (both print and non-print) in their subject area.

This includes the responsibility for long and short range planning.

Evaluation of campus collections and needs.

Regular communication with campus library staff.

Active liaison with their subject area faculty and administrators.

Judicious and timely expenditure of their materials budget.

Accurate record keeping and reporting of all collection development activities.

.1.5.3 It is the responsibility of the campus librarian (full and parttime) to work with the subject specialists in building and maintaining materials collections at their respective campus libraries that, within the concept of multicampus library interdependence and under budgetary and space restrictions, meet the educational needs of the students and the teaching needs of the faculty there:

By submitting orders for specific items based either on review sources or faculty and student requests.

Identifying and communicating general and specific collection needs.

Participating in weeding outdated and unneeded materials.

Informing the appropriate subject specialists of general faculty input.

Informing faculty of policies and procedures relating to materials selection and ordering.

Communicating information regarding changes in the nature of courses taught and student body at their campuses.

.1.6 Criteria for Selection of Materials

.1.6.1 The library selects print and non-print materials from a number of professional selection tools.

These include professional journals.

Popular review sources.

Standard bibliographies.

Publishers' and producers' catalogs.

Also from requests submitted by faculty, staff and students.

The library also accepts gift materials (see separate policy for gift materials).

.1.6.2 When selecting materials, an overriding consideration is appropriateness for community college use.

Most materials should be written or produced on a level that the average community college student can use or benefit from, or at a level that students in a particular field are expected to attain.

.1.6.3 Selection is also conditioned by the Library Bill of Rights (Appendix A) and the Freedom to Read Statement (Appendix B) as ratified by the American Library Association, and approved by the HCCS Board of Trustees (10-20-75).

.1.6.4 In addition to the above, the following criteria are used to evaluate materials considered for acquisition and inclusion in the collection.

Relevance to instructional needs.

Correlation to the existing collection.

Appropriateness of the medium/compatibility with hardware already owned.

Timeliness/permanence of contents.

Quality of writing.

Reputation of author, director, publisher, producer.

Scarcity of materials on subject matter.

Demand.

Age.

Cost in relatioı to other costs and other relevant materials.

Storage needs.

Availability elsewhere.

.1.6.5 Due to budgetary and space limitations and based on the goal of interdependence and shared resources among HCCS libraries, duplication of book titles is made judiciously and as need and demand absolutely require.

.1.6.6 Titles are not automatically purchased in large quantities or as single copies, but what seems to be the best combination of quantity and anticipated needs.

.1.6.7 Duplication of titles within the HCCS collection at any one location should be avoided. However, very heavy demand may mandate such duplication.

.1.6.8 Materials may be loaned or transferred from campus to campus, and this should be attempted before ordering permanent duplicates for any one campus.

.1.6.9 Purchase of materials for shared facility libraries should be carefully considered with regard to the "host" institution's collection and usage.

Subject specialists should become as familiar as possible with each campus collection, student body, and courses offered.

Consultation with the HCCS campus librarian and school librarian is urged, as well as continuing dialogue with instructors, department heads, instructional and campus administrators.

.1.7 Central Campus Library

.1.7.1 The Central Library has been established as the principal resource center for the system.

.1.7.2 It houses the largest book, periodical, and equipment collections in the system.

.1.7.3 It is also the home of the primary media collection, consisting of media in many formats on a wide spectrum of subjects for general use at all campuses.

.1.7.4 The Central Campus library serves the needs of the Central Campus population and as a backup and resource for all of the other campus libraries in the system.

.1.8 Campus Collection

.1.8.1 A major goal of collection development is to provide interdependence among the many campus libraries within the HCCS library system.

.1.8.2 Space and budget limitations preclude large independent collections at each campus library.

.1.8.3 Through knowledgeable, balanced selection and location of materials and the use of our catalog on microfiche, students and faculty have access to a much larger quantity and scope of materials than the collection found on any one campus could possibly provide.

.1.8.4 Each campus, however, is different, has its own unique needs and capabilities based on its courses, students, faculty, as well as its particular location and size, and, in case of shared facilities, its relationship to its "host" institution.

.1.8.5 Only specialized libraries with narrow, campus-specific needs such as Health Careers, Technical Education and the Auto Center have media collections of any size, and these are limited in subject matter.

.1.9 Materials Formats

.1.9.1 This section describes the various types of materials and formats purchased by the library.

.1.9.2 Print materials

.1.9.2.1 Books

Hardbound materials are preferred for inclusion in the cataloged collection.
If a choice is available between a hardbound or paper edition of the same title (and edition), the hardbound should be purchased, unless the cost difference is so great as to prohibit purchase in hardbound format.

Textbooks adapted for courses are not customarily purchased by the library. Subject specialists do, however, have the discretion to make exceptions to this.

Workbooks or any other work that consists primarily of pages to be filled in are considered consumables and are not purchased.

Paperbound materials may be purchased for inclusion in the collection if a hardbound edition is not available.

Mass market paperbacks are purchased for recreational reading. They are regarded as a browsing collection and are not cataloged or classified.

.1.9.2.2 Serials.

A serial is defined as a publication "issued in successive parts bearing numerical or chronological designations and intended to be continued indefinitely." (ALA Glossary, 1983) The Library recognizes four different categories of serials:

2.0 Public Services
2.3 Collection Development

Periodicals, also referred to as magazines or journals, are serials that are issued more frequently than annually.

Periodicals are purchased on a subscription basis for all libraries.

The library attempts to subscribe to periodicals through a jobber to simplify the ordering and payment process, and to insure that all subscriptions run concurrently on an annual basis.

Ordering - normally, subscriptions are done on an annual basis, running January-December. The major periodicals order is submitted for approval and processing August/September of the previous year, except in years (usually every third) when they must go out on bid for a jobber. When this occurs, orders must be ready for submission in June/July.

Requests for subscriptions should be received at least several weeks ahead of these deadlines, in order to assure their being processed.

Selection Criteria.

Recommendations about specific titles, numbers of copies and locations are made by the Central Services Librarian to the Coordinator of Public Services. These recommendations are based on information provided by campus librarians and subject specialists.

The quantity and specific titles at any one campus library depend on a number of variables: course offerings, enrollment, faculty and student requests, library use, space and budgetary limitations. The goal is to provide basic coverage at most campus libraries to support specific courses being taught as well as to provide both general interest and news magazines of international, national and local interest.

Libraries located in shared facilities usually do not duplicate periodical subscriptions received by the other sharing institution as long as these are available to HCCS students.

2.0 Public Services
2.3 Collection Development

Campus librarians are expected to work with the school librarians at these sites to insure that the subscriptions will complement each other, providing a more complete, well-rounded collection than would otherwise be possible.

Index coverage.

As a general rule, the library will not subscribe to periodicals that are not indexed in one or more of the indexes received by the library.

The library's aim is to maintain complete or near complete coverage of broad interest indexes and lesser coverage of more narrowly focused indexes, e.g. the library subscribes to nearly every periodical indexed in Readers Guide, but only to relatively few periodicals indexed in Criminal Justice Index.

Central Library

The system's most comprehensive periodical holdings are housed at Central. This collection is intended as a resource for the entire system.

Other libraries with specialized collections also maintain backfile holdings on microfiche.

Parttime campus libraries maintain limited hardcopy backfiles of titles received at their locations. The scope of these collections is dependent upon local needs and space considerations. These campuses are encouraged to use the backfiles at Central and the other specialized collections and are provided with regularly updated lists to facilitate this use.

Format.

Most titles are purchased in both hard and microform copies.

The hard copy is replaced by the microform when it becomes available. This is done either annually or, preferably, on a quarterly basis.

2.0 Public Services
2.3 Collection Development

Because of space and cost, some periodicals are only purchased in microform.

The preferred format is microfiche, although microfilm is acceptable for newspaper subscriptions and when fiche is not available. Negative vesicular (non-silver) 35 mm is the preferred type and size.

Processing - Periodicals are cataloged and appear in the catalog.

They are not, however, classified, but rather are shelved or stored in alphabetical title order on the shelf or in the storage cabinets.

Serials - Serials are publications issued in successive parts at an annual or lesser frequency. They include such items as almanacs, yearbooks, directories, etc.

Selection responsibility resides with the Coordinator of Public Services based on the same criteria and input used for periodical decisions.

Ordering - Similar to periodicals, they are ordered on an annual, calendar year basis.

Processing - Serials are both classified and cataloged and are shelved with the circulating and reference collection, as appropriate.

Weeding - Superceded volumes are either transferred to another location, moved from reference to the circulating collection or withdrawn. Decisions are made on a case by case basis.

Newspapers - A serial issued at stated, frequent intervals (daily, weekly or semiweekly) containing news, opinions, advertisements and other items of current, often local, interest.

For purposes of ordering, receiving, storing and retrieving current subscriptions and backfiles, newspapers are handled in the same manner as periodicals.

2.0 Public Services
2.3 Collection Development

Indexes - An alphabetical listing of names, subjects, etc. that indicates where to find a particular piece of information in a book, newspaper, journal, or magazine.

The selection and ordering process is handled in the same manner as serials and periodicals.

Indexes are both classified and cataloged and are shelved in the reference area.

Indexes are regularly updated by paper editions that are annually cumulated and replaced with a hardbound volume.

Weeding is seldom done so that the library can accumulate backfiles of where to find needed information.

Loose-leaf services - A serial that is revised, cumulated, or indexed by means of new or replacement pages inserted into a loose-leaf binder, and used where latest revisions of information are important.

Most are business sources covering a specific subject such as company financial information, laws, court decisions, new trends and development, etc. which change often.

They are generally treated as reference books, and are classified and shelved in the reference section.

Due to the high subscription costs, only one copy is usually acquired for the library system.

A subject specialist originates the order, usually in response to a faculty request.

Ordering - Loose-leaf services are normally ordered in the fall with the other serials, for a calendar-year subscription.

.1.9.3 Non-Print Materials

.1.9.3.1 Audio-visual software

Formats currently in use:

- Videocassette (1/2 VHS) (VTC)
- 16 MM Film (Film)
- Audiocassette (CAS)
- Slide/Cassette (SLC)
- Filmstrip/Cassette (FSC)
- Filmloop (FL)
- Slide (SLI)
- Filmstrip (FS)
- Kit
- Transparency (TRS)
- Map
- Game
- Phonograph record (PHO)
- Videodisk (VDD)

Selection criteria.

Software must be compatible with equipment owned by the library.

Caution is advised when considering the purchase of other than heavy-use formats such as videocassettes and 16mm films.

Whenever a choice is available, preference should be given to media which is closed captioned over media which is not closed captioned.

There should be a definite commitment by the requesting instructor to use these items. (See also .1.6 Criteria for Selection of materials).

Because of cost, software is ordered on a 'Preview' basis and must be previewed by faculty. Faculty must indicate a willingness to use media in the classroom as a precondition for purchase.

Items costing under $50 may be purchased outright.

Processing and shelving.

Media is fully cataloged and classified.

Each format is also assigned an accession number, based on receipt.

Media at Central is shelved separately from print materials and is arranged by accession number, rather than classification number.

Other campuses with media may either follow this arrangement or interfile media with the print collection.

Location - The primary media collection is housed at Central.

Other specialized campuses also maintain substantial media collections and a limited number of titles are housed at all sites.

.1.9.3.2 Microcomputer Software (CSOF)

Selection criteria.

Compatibility - Software must be compatible with hardware owned by the library.

Because of cost, software is ordered on a 'Preview' basis and must be previewed by faculty.

Faculty must indicate a willingness to use software in the classroom as a precondition for purchase.

General use items are also acquired to meet a number of needs:

Application/productivity programs to expedite specific tasks (e.g. word processing).

Teach specific subject content.

Teach microcomputer use skills.

Processing and shelving.

Software is fully cataloged and classified. Each format is also assigned an accession number, based on receipt.

Locations - The primary collection is housed at Central.

Other specialized campuses also maintain media collections. A restricted number of titles are housed at all sites.

.1.10 Weeding

Weeding is an integral and important aspect of the collection development/management process.
It is an ongoing process, reflecting changing needs and current developments in every area.

Responsibility for weeding rests with subject specialists and Campus Librarians, with the Subject Specialist taking the initiative and reviewing all materials.

The following are general guidelines that may be applied to the weeding process both generally and within each subject area. Subject Specialists may provide more specific guidelines in their areas as need indicates. The general guidelines are valid for print and non-print materials except where otherwise indicated.

Multiple copies - Generally there should not be more than one copy per title on any campus. Additional copies should be either reassigned or withdrawn. Exceptions are heavy use of a title, but this should be monitored closely, and as soon as the demand lessens, additional copies should be weeded.

Editions - In most cases, a later edition will replace an earlier edition of a work. When 2d, 3d, 4th, etc., editions are received, older editions should be examined closely and weeded if appropriate.

Erroneous or outdated information - especially applicable in the sciences and technical areas. Works that may contain out-of-date information should be weeded. This is an area where consultation with appropriate faculty may be necessary. Generally, works over five years old should be looked at carefully.

Discontinued programs or courses - print materials supporting programs or courses that are no longer offered on a particular campus or in the system should be examined for general relevance. Materials should be moved to the corresponding campus when a program or course moves, or may need to be withdrawn if areas are no longer covered at all by the system.

Use patterns - materials that have not been checked out for 4-5 years should be considered for withdrawal. For whatever reason these materials are not meeting students' needs.

Serials/Annuals - When newer editions of serials or annuals are received, the older editions should be withdrawn. Generally, these are reference materials, and

if the Librarians determine that the need exists, the older editions may be placed in the circulating collection, but these also should be withdrawn as they are replaced.

Textbooks - Although the library tries to avoid acquisition of textbooks, this is not always possible. However, all textbooks should be examined carefully whenever newer texts become available or when a course no longer uses a text or is no longer taught.

Age - Except in some areas of the humanities and social sciences materials of a certain age have a very limited value and should be withdrawn or replaced with new materials. Generally, any title over ten years old should be looked at carefully to determine its continuing value.

Physical condition - Materials that have been damaged or are missing some part should be either replaced or withdrawn entirely.

Level of materials - Level of materials should be that which is most accessible to student body. Advanced works may need to be replaced by more basic works appropriate to a community college setting or basic works may need to be replaced or supplemented by more in-depth, comprehensive coverage if the need exists.

Audiovisual media weeding should be done in conjunction with the appropriate instructional personnel.

.1.11 Gifts

The library is always pleased to receive donations of appropriate materials.

All donated materials are reviewed by pertinent subject specialists to determine usefulness to the collection.

Materials deemed not appropriate will either be returned, placed on the library's sale table, given to a non-profit agency or discarded.

Letters of acknowledgement will be sent to all donors, itemizing number of volumes received.

No monetary value will be placed on donations.

.1.12 **Budget Allocations**

This section discusses the way in which the materials budget is divided among the subject areas and within each subject area.

The initial budget allocation is given to the library by the upper administration.

.1.12.1 Once the materials budget is received, a number of initial allocations are decided upon.

An initial decision is made on how much to allocate to serials and periodicals.

This decision is based on current year costs, inflation, new locations, and backfile needs.

Additional allocations are made to:

- Government Printing Office Acct.
- Mass Market paperbacks
- Library Science
- Children and Youth Collection
- SIS
- Reserve Fund

Remaining funds are divided among the following Subject areas:

Arts & Humanities	Industrial Education
Business Careers	Math/Science
Consumer Services	Marketing & Management
Data Processing	Public Services Car.
Developmental Ed.	Social Sciences
Health Careers	Technical Education

Allocations are made based upon the following criteria:

- Number of campuses offering subject
- Total number of sections
- Headcount
- Library use intensive
- A-V use
- Cross disciplinary use
- Circulation

After receiving allocation, subject specialist divides the funds among the various departments in the area, and between anticipated expenditures for print and A-V materials.

Subject Specialists are responsible for three reports concerning budget allocation during the year.

Beginning of the year report
- Includes subject breakdown and print A-V breakdown
- Highlights goals and priorities for year
- Chronicles all meetings to date

Mid-year report -
- Record of expenditures to date
- Any changes in allocations
- Chronicle of meetings

End of the year report -
- Detailed record of all expenditures for year
- Chronicle of all meetings since mid-year report
- Narrative of major achievements and problems

.2 **Special Collections and Archives**

.2.1 The College and Library are pleased to accept all archival or special materials that substantively contribute to the realization of the library's mission to "supplement, support and enhance the educational process." Because of the special handling such materials often require, care will be taken to insure that only materials that will make a real contribution will be accepted.

.2.2 Generally gift items, collections or materials with a low dollar value and those requiring no special handling will be accepted by the library directly. These will be integrated into the library's general reference and circulating collections, provided that they meet the criteria of relevance to achieving the library's mission.

.2.3 Materials which are either of significant value or large collections that will require additional staff for the special storage, processing and security of the items, will need to be officially accepted by the Board of Trustees. Such acceptance implies a college commitment to provide sufficient space and staff to properly store, maintain and use the materials.

.2.4 These types of materials will constitute a "Special Collections" part of the library and be separated from the general collections of materials because of format, value and special conditions needed to maintain these materials.

.2.5 In considering such materials the following guidelines will be followed:

.2.5.1 Appraisal

Before accepting special collections the Board with the assistance of either or both internal or external experts, will perform an appraisal to determine:

.2.5.1.1 Relevance to the needs of the college community in the achievement of its mission. Materials that are accepted should clearly relate to and significantly support student and faculty needs.

.2.5.1.2 Special requirements that will be needed to properly maintain the collection, including space, environmental control, security, special processing, and staff, as well as a cost estimate for these.

.2.5.1.3 An appraisal of value of the materials to determine whether to insure the collection.

.2.5.2 Acceptance

Acceptance by the Board should include a Deed of Gift from the current owner to insure that no questions of ownership arise.

Deed of Gift should include:

.2.5.2.1 Any use restrictions

.2.5.2.2 Any copyright restrictions

.2.5.2.3 Requirements concerning maintenance of the collection and restrictions on possible subsequent dispersal.

.2.5.3 Storage

Acceptance of a collection by the Board will imply a commitment to provide adequate storage space, which will meet proper temperature, humidity and security requirements.

Staff trained in handling special collections will be hired to process and catalog the materials, and to create a useable index for use by students and scholars.

.2.6 Accessibility

Materials will be made available to all students and staff of HCCS and to others who have a legitimate scholarly interest in the materials (as determined by either the appropriate department head or library director).

Copies of materials may be made, depending on copyright restrictions.

Title MATERIALS SELECTION Number VI-23

Legal Authority By approval of the Board of Trustees Page 1 of 9

Approval, Board of Trustees ~~July 7, 1980, as amended March 9, 1987,~~ September 14, 1992

Policy

A. Introduction and Purpose

1. ACC offers freshman and sophomore arts and sciences courses, occupational programs, avocational and vocational continuing education courses, and adult basic education.

2. Learning Resource Services (LRS) provides the educational resources necessary to support the goals of Austin Community College (ACC). Educational resources refers to instructional, enrichment, and training materials in varied formats chosen to reflect the purpose of the College, courses offered, varied teaching methods, and special needs of the students, faculty and staff.

3. LRS recognizes and seeks to serve a diverse clientele who are varied in age, literacy level, ethnic background, and previous exposure to formal education.

B. Availability of Materials

LRS seeks to provide a sufficient and useful multimedia collection for all programs and divisions of the College. LRS attempts to provide a timely collection that is relevant, vital, and useful. LRS does not seek to build a comprehensive or research collection in any one subject area.

C. Responsibility for Materials Selection

1. Subject selection specialists are responsible for collection development in terms of coordinating and balancing the collection as a whole.

President ______ Date ______

Policy

2. Full and part-time faculty and all college staff are encouraged to take professional responsibility to make materials recommendations in their area of expertise.

3. The Director of LRS is responsible for final purchase decisions based on the criteria outlined in the "General Criteria for Selection."

D. Materials Considered for Acquisition

1. Subject matter that is directly curriculum-related is considered first for acquisition. This includes items needed for class assignments, supplemental materials, reference materials, and bibliographic tools which will facilitate finding and using such materials.

2. After primary needs have been met, consideration will be given to materials which meet special needs or interests of students, faculty, and staff.

E. Materials Not Considered for Acquisition

The following types of materials are generally not considered for acquisition:

1. Required textbooks and lab manuals;

2. Specialized technical books or research materials beyond the needs of the students;

3. Rare materials, or limited editions;

4. Materials which will not be easily accessible to most students;

Title MATERIALS SELECTION Number VI-23

Legal Authority By approval of the Board of Trustees Page 3 of 9

Approval, Board of Trustees July 7, 1980, as amended March 9, 1987, September 14, 1992

Policy

5. Audiovisual materials that are cost-prohibitive to purchase and can be rented for a reasonable price;

6. Foreign language material except those that support ACC foreign language classes;

7. Out-of-print materials are purchased under special circumstances only.

F. General Criteria for Selection

1. Printed materials are selected on the basis of:

    -- instructional support
    -- critiques appearing in standard selection periodicals and tools
    -- faculty review and recommendation
    -- non-availability in current collection
    -- demand and potential use
    -- significance
    -- permanence
    -- timeliness
    -- cost commensurate with quality and potential benefit
    -- inclusion in indexes available at the college and in standard lists and bibliographies
    -- program accreditation requirements
    -- budget availability

2. In addition, computer software and audiovisual materials are selected also on the basis of:

    -- overall technical quality and instructional design
    -- availability and compatibility of equipment

Title MATERIALS SELECTION Number VI-23

Legal Authority By approval of the Board of Trustees Page 4 of 9

Approval, Board of Trustees July 7, 1980, as amended March 9, 1987, September 14, 1992

Policy

-- the College's potential to produce better or less costly materials
-- the cost of computer software or audiovisual materials purchase in relation to rental

3. Microforms are selected for their permanent value and usefulness, as well as to meet equipment, storage and cost considerations.

4. Periodicals are selected to provide current information not readily available in other formats, to supplement the materials collection, to meet curriculum requirements or enhance curriculum offerings, to provide current information, to serve as reviewing and selection aides, and, occasionally, to provide recreational reading. Selection criteria for periodicals also include: preference for indexing or abstracting in college-owned reference sources, demonstrated need, reputation and price.

5. Newspapers are selected to represent local, state, and national news coverage and provide current information.

6. Pamphlets, catalogs, maps, newspaper clippings, pictures, and other ephemeral materials are selected for the collection on the basis of usefulness and are not generally catalogued into the collection. A pamphlet file has been established to organize these materials. A picture file is also available at some locations.

7. Machine-readable information sources (on-line data bases) are selected to provide appropriate additional, or alternative, methods of investigating data sources and accessing information not readily available in the regular collection.

Title MATERIALS SELECTION Number VI-23

Legal Authority By approval of the Board of Trustees Page 5 of 9

Approval, Board of Trustees July 7, 1980, as amended March 9, 1987, September 14, 1992

Policy

8. Popular paperback books are selected primarily as supplemental and/or recreational material and are minimally cataloged for the circulating collection.

9. Leisure reading materials are selected through a commercial rental/purchase plan and provide high interest/best seller titles for supplemental and/or recreational reading. Materials are selected from company lists by all bibliographers, on the basis of popular fiction and non-fiction content. Following use, return or purchase decisions are made by the bibliographers and then materials are withdrawn and sent back to the company or permanently added to the collection. This rental/purchase meets high demand needs with minimal supplemental/recreational budgets.

10. Special collections of materials may exist in the college. Learning Resource Services bibliographers and/or mediographers may be involved in the selection, acquisition, organization and housing of materials in a variety of ways. These ways could include, but are not limited to:

- selection of materials based on LRS criteria and special user needs
- acquisition and organization of materials
- cataloging of materials
- addition of materials to the LRS automated public access catalog database

- integrated shelving/housing of materials in a Learning Resource Center

- collection maintenance which includes repair, weeding and replacement.

G. Gifts

The same selection standards apply to gifts as to the rest of the collection. The LRS reserves the right to refuse materials and/or to dispose of any materials after acceptance which do not meet its needs or requirements according to stated College policy for disposition of materials. The College does not independently verify the stated value nor is it able to list titles donated, but may respond to the donor with a thank-you letter verifying the number of documents donated.

H. Maintenance of the Collection

1. Collection Maintenance and Evaluation

An essential element of collection maintenance is the systematic and periodic weeding of all formats of materials from the collection. Weeding is an evaluation mechanism as it maintains the purposes and quality of resources; increases the speed of access to materials, provides for accuracy in retrieval of materials, and increases the use of the collection. Weeding requires the same degree of attention as initial selection. Faculty are encouraged to assist in spotting outdated or inaccurate materials in their areas of expertise.

Title MATERIALS SELECTION Number VI-23

Legal Authority By approval of the Board of Trustees

Approval, Board of Trustees ~~July 7, 1980, as amended March 9, 1987,~~ September 14, 1992

Policy

Materials are withdrawn on the basis of:

-- Outdated information
-- Inaccuracy of content
-- Obsolescence of formats
-- Shortage of space
-- High cost of storing materials (e.g., cleaning, shelving, repair, climate)
-- Inappropriate volume count, content, format (e.g., curriculum ended/changed)
-- Use patterns (e.g., no use, low use)
-- Institutional issues and program criteria (e.g., program accreditation, sole technology commitment as only VHS)
-- Incomplete materials (e.g., book/software set with book missing, AV kit with pieces missing, mutilation)
-- Permissibility issues (e.g., licensing, copyright)
-- Level of treatment (e.g., too difficult, too easy)
-- Expert opinion (e.g., reviews, faculty input)
-- Materials damaged beyond repair, poor physical quality of format (e.g., bad tape, mutilation, mold)
-- Incompatibility of format to equipment available
-- Inaccessible information (e.g., periodicals not indexed)

2. Lost Items and Replacement

Resources that are missing, lost, or withdrawn because of wear are not automatically replaced. Materials which are known to be lost are replaced based on the following criteria:

-- Importance of the item to the collection
-- Demand for the material

-- Availability of materials in subject area
-- Availability of funds

3. Conservation, Preservation and Restoration

The LRS strives to maintain the physical integrity of materials in the collection through conservation measures such as temperature, humidity and dust control. Material will be repaired, rebound or reformatted when possible to preserve the content for continued use.

4. Remote Storage

Storing materials at locations other than open access LRC main campus, campus or site locations may be necessary. These remote location materials may be identified by LRS bibliographers based on these criteria:

- low use titles/volumes
- materials from locations with inadequate shelving space
- materials waiting to be sent to the bindery
- materials waiting for in-house repair
- materials with content of historical value to college programs.

Stored materials are retained in the public access catalog database and continue to be available to the college's students, faculty, administration and staff through the college's delivery system.

I. Intellectual Freedom Statement

The LRS staff supports the American Library Association's Bill of Rights and its concept of intellectual freedom. The LRS attempts to purchase materials which represent differing points of view on controversial matters. Subjects will be considered without prejudice or censorship when determining the balance of the collection as long as they fit into the general collection criteria of the LRS.

LEARNING RESOURCES CENTER
PROCEDURE

TITLE Cedar Valley College
DALLAS COM COL SYSTEM

COLLECTION DEVELOPMENT POLICY

Date	Page	Approved	Time
Dec 13, 1991	1 Of 6	[illegible]	

Responsibility	Action
	GOALS OF THE LIBRARY
	To provide: 1. material required for the successful completion of coursework offered by Cedar Valley College. 2. additional material via District intercampus loan. 3. access to material through AHE membership and interlibrary loan. 4. material for general or special professional growth. 5. material to advance cultural enrichment 6. material for extracurricular interests
	POLICY
FACULTY AND LIBRARY STAFF	Collection development is a combined effort of the library staff and the college faculty.
	Most purchases are restricted to titles in English, reference works and those supporting the curriculum. Other restrictions are:
	TEXTBOOKS: Purchased only when they are the only source of needed information.
	PROFESSIONAL: Purchased if they relate to subjects of campus concern.
	GENERAL NEED: Items of greater need are purchased first.
	The collection reflects a variety of viewpoints on controversial subjects. This is to enable students to practice critical reading and thinking skills.
	The library staff can anticipate needs only in a limited way. Instructors should verify the availability of resources in the library before making class assignments.

LEARNING RESOURCES CENTER
PROCEDURE

TITLE

COLLECTION DEVELOPMENT POLICY

Date	Page	Approved	Time
Dec 13, 1991	2 Of 6		

Responsibility	Action
	Print material is included in the collection when the following evaluative criteria is met: 1. importance of subject matter to curriculum 2. permanent or timely value 3. competent and qualified author, editor or compiler 4. accuracy of information 5. readability 6. reputation and professional standing of publisher 7. price 8. format 9. availability of material elsewhere in community 10. scarcity of material available 11. interest by student or faculty 12. historical value
	Serial publications are included in the collection when one or more of the following criteria is met: 1. importance of title to the curriculum 2. scarcity of materials in other formats 3. indexing in standard indexes 4. presentation on the community college students' reading and interest level 5. availability of back issues on microfilm 6. number of journals received in the subject area 7. price
	Non-print material that meet one or more of the following evaluative criteria may be considered for inclusion in the collection: 1. enrichment and support to the curriculum 2. appropriateness for age, intelligence, abilities and interest of students 3. technical and artistic quality 4. authority of producer 5. contribution of uniqueness or significance by the presentation or content 6. price 7. availability of material in other formats 8. scarcity of material available 9. interest by student or faculty

LEARNING RESOURCES CENTER
PROCEDURE

TITLE

COLLECTION DEVELOPMENT POLICY

Date	Page	Approved	Time
Dec 13, 1991	3 Of 6		

Responsibility	Action
	QUESTIONED MATERIAL The Learning Resources Center does not add or withdraw, at the request of any individual or group, material which has been chosen or excluded on the basis of stated selection criteria. Any individual or group questioning the appropriateness of material in the collection should direct the question to the Dean of Educational Resources, LRC. A standard form and procedure for handling questioned material exists and should be completed by the patron for each objection (refer to "Procedures for Handling Questioned Materials").
LIBRARIAN	**STATEMENT OF GIFTS** The library will consider gifts of books and other materials on the individual merit of each item. The same criteria which applies to selection of material for the collection applies to gifts. The library staff reserves the right to reject any material on the basis of our stated selection policy. The library staff will not make appraisals of materials either for re-sale value or statements of donation on income tax reports. A letter of acknowledgment will be sent to the donor. (Refer to Section 14 of the DCCCD Business Office Procedures Manual for specific procedures).
LRC STAFF	**MAINTENANCE OF THE COLLECTION** The LRC will retain control of all resources purchased through its budget and placed in its inventory.
LIBRARIAN	**MULTIPLE COPIES** Duplicate copies of material are held to minimum at all times. Need for duplicates are determined by utilization, importance or material to curriculum, budget, and price.
LIBRARIAN	**REPLACEMENT OF LOST OR DAMAGED MATERIAL** For lost or damaged material, the same general and specific criteria for selection will apply if the material is placed in the collection.

LEARNING RESOURCES CENTER
PROCEDURE

TITLE

COLLECTION DEVELOPMENT POLICY

Date	Page	Approved	Time
Dec 13, 1991	4 Of 6		

Responsibility	Action
LIBRARY STAFF AND FACULTY	**WEEDING** Systematic withdrawals are conducted of outdated, damaged, and worn material no longer useful. Withdrawn materials are sent to the Technical Services Center for appropriate disposition. The following criteria are considered when discarding material: 1. obsolescence 2. physical condition 3. insufficient use or basic value 4. changing curricular needs
DEAN OF EDUCATIONAL RESOURCES	Policy Review The Dean of Educational Resources should review this Materials Selection Policy periodically and make recommended changes to the Director of Instructional Resources.

LEARNING RESOURCES CENTER PROCEDURE			TITLE COLLECTION DEVELOPMENT POLICY
Date Dec 13, 1991	Page 5 Of 6	Approved	Time

Responsibility	Action
	PROCEDURES FOR HANDLING QUESTIONED MATERIALS
PATRON	1. When a complaint is received, the patron is referred to the Dean of Educational Resources Learning Resources Center. If the Dean is unavailable, the patron's name, phone number and mailing address is noted.
DEAN OF EDUCATIONAL RESOURCES	2. The Dean is informed of the complaint as soon as possible.
	3. The Dean contacts patron to set up meeting. During the meeting the following procedures should be followed: a. Allow the patron to speak freely without interruption. b. Discuss the objections with the patron and explain the basic philosophy contained in the materials selection policy. c. Ask the patron for recommendations regarding the material referring to the LRC policy and procedure in this situation. d. If the explanation does not satisfy the patron, a copy of the Patron Objection to Materials Form should be completed. The patron may take the form home and return it by mail to the Dean. e. No commitment is made by the Dean at this time. Appropriate campus administration is informed.
VICE-PRESIDENT OF INSTRUCTION	4. The Dean then informs the Vice President of Instruction, who calls an ad hoc committee comprised of: Vice President of Instruction, Dean of Educational Resources, Director of Instructional Resources, two faculty members from the appropriate divisions, and one Professional Support Staff member.
AD HOC COMMITTEE	5. This committee will review the complaint in consideration with the basic philosophy contained in the materials selection policy and the DCCCD philosophy.
	6. The committee's decision will be in the form of a written letter to the patron.

DALLAS COUNTY COMMUNITY COLLEGE DISTRICT

Patron Objection to LRC Materials

Please complete the following concerning the material in question and return to:

Dean of Educational Resources
Cedar Valley College
Learning Resources Center
Lancaster, Texas 75134-3799

Format (book, record, film, tape, etc.): ____________

Author: ____________

Title: ____________

Producer or Publisher: ____________

Patron's Name: ____________

Telephone: ____________

Address: ____________

City: ____________ Zip code: ____________

1. Do you represent an organization? ________ If so, please identify it. ____________

2. Have you read, seen or heard this material in its entirety? ______ If not, which parts? ____________

3. To what in this material did you object? (Please be specific; if printed material, cite pages) ____________

4. Do you believe there is anything good about this material? ____________

5. Are you familiar with reviews of this material? ____________

6. Can you recommend an alternate to this material? ____________

____________ (date) ____________ (patron's signature)

Note to patron: Your concern is appreciated. Your objection will be referred to the appropriate committee. You will receive a written response concerning their decision as soon as possible.

The following list represents specific periodical titles assigned to library staff:

SCIENCE/AMT - DAVA STEPHENS

1. American Biology Teacher
2. Anthrozoos
3. BioScience
4. Bulletin of the Atomic Scientists
5. Environment
6. Journal of the American Veterinary Medical Assoc.
7. Science (Book Issue)
8. Scientific American
9. Technology Review
10. VM/SAC

ENGLISH/SOCIOLOGY/HISTORY/GENERAL - JEFF STAGNER

1. American Historical Review
2. American Journal of Sociology
3. College English
4. English Journal
5. Modern Language Quarterly
6. Modern Fiction Studies
7. Progressive
8. Western American Literature
9. Utne Reader
10. U. S. News and World Report

HISTORY/SCIENCE/EDUCATION/GENERAL - KIM ROSS

1. America
2. American Libraries
3. American Scholar
4. Booklist
5. Chronicle of Higher Education
6. Journal of American History
7. Natural History
8. Perspective
9. Smithsonian
10. Newsweek

ART/BUSINESS/GENERAL - EDNA WHITE

1. American Artist
2. American Craft
3. Commentary
4. Community, Technical and Junior College Journal
5. College and Research Libraries News
6. Harvard Business Review
7. Hispanic Business
8. Humanist
9. Time
10. USA Today

MATERIAL SELECTION

Selection of print and non-print material is a multi-faceted procedure. It permeates the entire fabric of a library. Librarians are constantly selecting material, consciously or unconsciously, whether reading at work or home. The following is the more formalized method we use at Cedar Valley College.

1. Memos
   a. to faculty, full-time and part-time
   b. administrators

2. Reading lists

3. Read reviews
   a. Professional journals, e.g. <u>Booklist</u>, <u>Choice</u>
   b. current events periodicals, e.g. <u>Time</u>, <u>Newsweek</u>
   c. <u>Choice</u> cards
   d. publishers catalogs, brochures
   e. newspapers, e.g. <u>Chronicle of Higher Education</u>

4. Check bibliographies and indexes against collection
   a. order Pulitzer prize-winning books
   b. <u>Short Story Explication</u>
   c. Indexes:
      <u>Essay and General Literature Index</u>
      <u>Poetry Explication</u>

5. Personal contact
   a. contact instructor teaching a new course when possible
   b. talk to instructors we do library instruction classes for
   c. request reading lists and syllabi from Division Deans

6. Demand
   a. requests made by faculty/staff
   b. requests made by students for assignments

7. Intercampus/Interlibrary loans
   books requested three times yearly are ordered

8. Discussion among library staff in the planning process
   Perceived need for specific library resources to update or add to the collection

NON-PRINT MATERIAL - JUDY MCMULLAN

1. PBS Video
2. Educational Video Network, Inc.
3. Insight Media
4. Films for the Humanities & Sciences
5. Learning Seed
6. Film Archives
7. Guidance Associates, The Center for Humanities
8. Cambridge Video
9. Coronet/MTI Film & Video
10. Sunburst Communications

COPPER MOUNTAIN CAMPUS LIBRARY COLLECTION DEVELOPMENT POLICY

I. INTRODUCTION

The purpose of a collection development policy is to clearly state the principles and guidelines along which the process of selecting and acquiring library materials will proceed. It is useful both in providing consistency among those who have responsibility for developing the collection, and in communicating the library's policies to faculty, students and other members of the college community. It is understood that as the programs and other information needs of the college change so the collection development policy must be altered by the standing CMC Library Committee to meet these changing needs. All members of the college community are encouraged to contribute their ideas concerning the nature and content of the collection development policy.

II. MISSION OF THE LIBRARY

The mission of the Copper Mountain Campus Library is to provide up to date, comprehensive information to support the College's academic curriculum. First, the library's purpose is to supply services and materials for students and faculty. Second, the library serves the greater desert community, its citizens, alumni and friends of the area. The library through its staff works with administrators and the community to meet information needs through its collection and varied services.

III. RESPONSIBILITY FOR COLLECTION DEVELOPMENT

While the library has ultimate responsibility for collection development, faculty, staff and students of the college are encouraged to contribute to the building of the library's collection. Every effort will be made to accommodate faculty requests that are within the scope of the library's collection development policy. The Librarian supervises the collection development process.

IV. GENERAL GUIDELINES FOR ACQUISITIONS

Major criteria for acquisitions include:

1. High quality of scholarship, content format and literary merit.
2. Permanent value.
3. Currency and timeliness of the information.
4. Appropriateness for lower-division college use.
5. Balance of current holdings - representative materials on all sides of an issue.
6. Value as a classic or outstanding work in a field.

Additional criteria for books:

1. Positive reviews of the work in sources important to the field.
2. Reputation and credibility of author in the subject area.
3. Fiction should be selected with an emphasis on its use in the formal study of literature or its impact on social and political thought, philosophical ideas, and wider values.
4. Hardcover editions should be preferred over paperbacks.
5. Textbooks adopted for classroom use should not be purchased unless they are classics in the field. This criterion does not exclude other monographs selected by instructors for classroom assignments.
6. In general, the library does not acquire multiple copies of materials. Multiple copies of faculty requests or receipt of gifts of popular titles may be added.

Additional criteria for serials:

Because of limited library funds, selection of serials must be especially careful; if a new serial is ordered, the intention is to retain it as a permanent part of the collection in an complete a run as possible. In addition to the general criteria for library acquisitions, serials should be chosen with the following specific requirements in mind:

1. Journals of an academic nature are preferred over popular or general magazines.
2. Journals which do not support a specific element of the curriculum may be purchased if they contribute to the general liberal education of students by presenting an informed discussion of public affairs, economic, social, or political events, scientific or technical knowledge, literature, criticism, or the arts.
3. Serials which serve entertainment purposes only will not be purchased.
4. Serials which are not indexed in a major index carried by CMC Library will generally not be purchased. Newspapers and local history materials are exceptions to this policy.

V. GIFT POLICY

Gifts are accepted only when they add strength to the collection and impose no significant limitations on housing, handling, or disposition of duplicate or damaged items. Guidelines for evaluation of gifts are the same as those for selecting purchased materials. Library personnel will not issue appraisals of gift materials for tax or any other purpose. If there is any question about accepting a gift, the final determination rests with the Librarian.

VI. MAINTENANCE OF THE COLLECTION

WEEDING:

Weeding is the withdrawing of damaged or obsolete materials from the library's collection, a process which is an integral part of collection management. In general, the same criteria apply to weeding as apply to the selection of new materials. It is the responsibility of the library staff, in cooperation with the faculty, to withdraw materials which are inappropriate or damaged. The final disposal of all materials shall be approved by the Librarian. The decision to withdraw materials is based on the following criteria:

1. Superseded editions; unless previous edition is still of value.
2. Worn, mutilated, or badly marked items.
3. Duplicate copies of seldom-used items.
4. Materials which are outdated or inaccurate.
5. Circulation record of an item.

LOST ITEMS AND REPLACEMENTS:

Resources that are missing, lost, or withdrawn because of wear are not automatically replace. Materials which are known to be lost are replaced based on the following criteria:

1. Importance of the item to the collection.
2. Demand for the material.
3. Availability.

A search for missing materials is conducted for up to one year. Materials not found during that time period are declared lost and replacement is based on the above criteria. If there is high demand for a missing items, a second copy will be ordered immediately while the search is continued.

VII. ACADEMIC FREEDOM

In accordance with the American Library Association Bill of Rights and the American Library Association Freedom to Read Statement, the library collection attempts to provide for the free exchange of ideas. The collection is available to all potential patrons of the library, and should offer the widest possible range of viewpoints; regardless of the popularity of these viewpoints, or of the sex, religion, political philosophy, or national origin of the author.

No censorship will be exercised on the basis of frankness of language, or the controversial manner an author may use in dealing with religious, political, sexual, social, economic, scientific, or moral issues.

In handling criticisms of material or attempts at censorship, the Librarian will reply verbally or in writing to the person or group, quoting or referring to the above policy. Persistent or repeated criticisms from persons or groups will be referred to the college administration.

Appendix A. ALA Bill of Rights
Appendix B. ALA Freedom to Read Statement
Appendix C. Educational Film Library Freedom to View Statement

Policy approved 5/17/93, by the CMC Library Committee.

CHIPPEWA VALLEY TECHNICAL COLLEGE
TECHNOLOGY RESOURCE LIBRARY

COLLECTION MANAGEMENT GUIDELINES

I. RESPONSIBILITY FOR MATERIAL SELECTION

The overall goal of balanced collection development will be under the direction of the Library Services Manager, in consultation with the Chippewa Valley Technical College Faculty and staff.

The CVTC Technology Resource Library is committed to an integrated, unified approach to collection development, organization and service. To accomplish this, the staff will:

A. Acquire materials which support CVTC's academic mission by following an established collection development policy.

Collection Development Priorities are:

1. To support the curriculum of each program/service area with current, accurate materials.

2. To provide a professional education and/or management collection for faculty and staff.

3. To provide current professional materials for faculty/staff in technological fields where rapid change is the norm.

4. To provide materials in support of the remedial academic basic skills program.

5. To provide general resources in the following areas:

   a. career/job vocational information
   b. information for citizenship
   c. consumer information for life, literacy, financial concerns
   d. enrichment and recreation materials

B. Provide equal learning opportunities for all users by acquiring these resources in all types of media formats.

C. Organize the materials collection and provide efficient retrieval systems that will enhance their utilization.

D. Provide bibliographic instruction in use of library resources, facilities or services for orientation and/or introductory purposes or for curricular instruction.

E. Establish equitable loan policies to encourage maximum use of library resources, facilities and services.

F. Staff the library with individuals who are committed to providing quality customer service.

G. Promote awareness of library resources and services through appropriate CVTC channels/publications.

H. Keep CVTC faculty/staff current with latest developments and/or trends relating to information access in academic libraries by participation in state, national professional library and academic activities.

II. CRITERIA FOR MATERIAL SELECTION

Materials will also be selected based on the following additional parameters:

A. **General information** - balanced learning requires general information resources in subject areas not necessarily covered by classroom instruction. Support for balanced learning means materials shall be chosen that provide information about all spectrums of our culturally diverse society along with materials that represent all the roles and lifestyles for both women and men in today's information age.

B. **Language** - material will be collected primarily in the English language.

C. **New curricula** - the Technology Resource Library must maintain the flexibility to develop collections in new program areas as well as expand existing subject collections to meet curriculum changes.

D. **CVTC history** - printed and audiovisual materials relating to the history and development of the college will be maintained as an archives special collection.

E. **Shared resources** - holdings of other libraries in this local area as well as the possibility of sharing through interlibrary loan will be a factor in decisions to purchase expensive acquisitions.

F. **Reserve materials** - only one copy will be purchased for reserve purposes, any additional copies will be the responsibility of the requesting department.

G. **Textbooks** - in most subject areas, books used as texts for courses will not be acquired for permanent holdings.

H. **Multiple copies** - as a standard practice, only one copy of a title will be purchased for the circulating collection.

I. **Balancing media types** - all types of media will be considered resource materials for this collection. These formats which include print, audiovisual and computer software, as well as other emerging electronic formats, will be acquired, organized and maintained in a balanced structure.

III. COLLECTION DEVELOPMENT LEVELS

Utilizing the Library of Congress Classification system as a structure, the following collecting levels will be used as a guideline for subject area materials acquisition in the library collection.

COLLECTING LEVELS:

0 - **Out of scope**: The Library does not collect in this area.

1 - **Minimal Level**: A subject area in which few selections are made beyond very basic or introductory works.

2 - **Basic Information Level**: A collection of up-to-date general materials that serves to introduce and define a subject and to indicate the varieties of information available elsewhere. It may include dictionaries, encyclopedias, selected editions of important works, historical survey, bibliographies, handbooks and other reference tools, a few major periodicals, in the minimum number that will serve the purpose. It is an adequate level to support courses requiring minimal library use.

3 - **Initial Study Level**: A collection which is adequate to support diploma level courses. It includes a selection of both current and retrospective books, a broad selection of works of more important writers; a selection of major journals; and current editions of the most significant reference tools and bibliographies pertaining to the subject.

4 - **Advanced Study Level**: A collection which is adequate to support associate degree courses; sustained independent study; and/or advanced certificate programs. It includes a wide range of basic books both current and retrospective, collections of the works of more important writers, selections from the works of secondary writers, a collection of journals supporting faculty teaching interests and local curricular strengths as well as various general aspects of the subject, and the reference and fundamental bibliographic tools pertaining to the subject.

IV. SELECTION OF SERIALS

The increasing number of periodicals currently published necessitates selectivity as budget growth has not kept pace with increasing cost and demand. Justification for specific new serial titles should be documented. The following guidelines are considered for purchasing additional titles to be added to the collection:

A. Periodicals listed in major highly used indexes that CVTC subscribes to.

B. Periodicals which are basic to CVTC mission and curriculum.

C. Continued use of the periodical once it is in the collection.

D. Frequency of Interlibrary Loan Requests.

All divisions will assign purchase priorities to the requested titles in the annual budgeting process. Periodical title retention will be evaluated annually.

V. NEWSPAPER SELECTION

Newspapers will be acquired on a current basis to meet the teaching and general information needs of CVTC patrons. Local newspapers from the district will be purchased along with selected titles representing major regional cities and several national newspapers. Due to storage space limitations, however, back issues of many newspapers will be kept for only short time periods unless retrospective issues are purchased in alternative formats requiring less storage space.

VI. PAMPHLETS

Pamphlets are acquired to supplement other library materials resources. This material is selected from numerous library reviewing sources as well as the Vertical File Index.

VII. WEEDING GUIDELINES

Deacquisition, or weeding of obsolete materials, is an integral part of the total collection maintenance process. The purpose of weeding is to evaluate the library collection as part of an on going annual process, each year discarding those materials that do not meet the established selection standards. The systematic removal of materials no longer useful is essential to maintaining the purposes and quality of the resources. This process keeps the collection current, functional and in support of the Technology Resource Library mission.

The primary responsibility for withdrawing resources lies with the Library Services Manager in consultation with CVTC faculty and staff. Decisions for actual material withdrawals are based on the established weeding criteria developed by cooperation with faculty and staff advisory committees. An adaption of the "Crew Method" has been modified to apply to weeding the CVTC collection.

A. **Deacquisition Guidelines:**

1. Works containing information which has become obsolete, have been superseded by newer editions, have inaccurate information, or have been cumulated in more comprehensive publications.

2. Duplicate/surplus copies of standard works no longer in demand for supplementary use.

3. Worn out or extensively marked books which cannot be easily repaired or rebound.

4. Broken files of unindexed journals, or journals no longer needed for curricular purposes.

5. Withdrawal of materials should not tend to bias the collection in favor or against any one viewpoint.

6. Adequacy of similar materials.

7. Lack of adequate storage space for materials, especially periodicals.

B. **Disposition of Withdrawn Materials**

The disposition of withdrawn materials will be in accordance with approved CVTC guidelines. After these procedures have been followed, then disposal shall be determined by its usefulness to the following:

1. CVTC faculty, staff and students

2. Local area libraries (academic, public, school) when appropriate.

3. Remote libraries through American Library Association or other exchange mechanism.

VIII. REPLACEMENT PROCEDURES

Titles which are lost, damaged or for which the last copy has been withdrawn are considered for replacement. The following criteria are applied:

A. Continued value of the particular work.

B. Existing coverage of the subject.

C. Availability of newer or better materials on the subject.

IX. GIFT POLICY

The Technology Resource Library encourages gifts and donations of useful library materials or the money donated through the CVTC Foundation to purchase them. However, all gifts of materials are accepted with the understanding that they are added to the collection only after they have met the same selection criteria as the materials which are to be purchased.

The Library will not accept gifts with conditions as to their disposition or location except by the express permission of the Library Services Manager. The Library retains the right to dispose of any material regardless of how it was acquired and will use the same procedure for discarding withdrawn materials. The Library can not legally appraise gifts for tax or inheritance purposes.

There are certain materials which are unsuitable for gifts, although the Library reserves the right to make exceptions whenever circumstances warrant:

A. Older editions of titles already owned by the Library.

B. Consumable materials, including workbooks, laboratory manuals and standardized tests.

C. Outdated titles.

D. Marked up or worn out materials.

E. Broken or defective runs of periodicals, unless the acquisition would complete an existing run.

F. Most ephemeral and mundane gifts which might result from spring house and/or office cleaning.

X. RECONSIDERATION OF MATERIALS

Reconsideration of library resources will be handled by the Library Services Manager upon receiving a written request from the patron and after the Reconsideration Request form has been filled out.

A reconsideration committee of three (3) members will be named by the Library Service Manager to consider the request. Their recommendation will be given to the Library Service Manager within two weeks (10 working days). They will consult the Technology Resource Library Guidelines and the Library Bill of Rights and other relative documents including book reviews when available.

The final decision on the disposition of the material being reconsidered will rest with the Library Services Manager in consultation with the CVTC Administrative Council and CVTC Board of Directors. The patron will be notified in writing when a decision has been reached. The material under question will remain on the shelves of the Technology Resource Library until a decision is reached.

Policy and/or Procedure: COLLECTION MANAGEMENT GUIDELINES	
Initiator/Date: E.Emberson 11/11/89	Reviewed Date:
Effective Date: 11/11/89	Revised Date: 02/26/92

POLICY\COMP_COL.MGT

EXPLANATORY NOTES

--/--/MUSTY = How old/How long in years since circulated/

MUSTY:
- Misleading
- Ugly
- Superceded (New edition)
- Trivial (Old best sellers)
- Your collection
- # of copies?

CHIPPEWA VALLEY TECHNICAL COLLEGE TECHNOLOGY RESOURCE LIBRARY

COLLECTION DEVELOPMENT

SAMPLE OF COLLECTION CONSPECTUS

LC CLASS #	LC DESCRIPTION	CREW FORMULA (XX/XX/MUSTY & NOTES):	COLLECTING LEVEL (CL): 0-4	DIVISION/DEPARTMENT/FACULTY/STAFF	CORE LISTS[1] (AUTHOR/SUBJECT/EDITION):
A	General works	10/--/MUSTY Stagger levels - Need latest; store historic	CL:1	All	
B	Psychology/Philosophy/Religion	10/05/MUSTY	CL:1	General Studies/Social Studies/M.Carlson	
BD	Philosophy	" "	CL:1		
BF	Applied & developmental	" "	CL:3	General Studies/Social Studies/M.Carlson	
BH-BJ	Aesthetics, ethics, etiquette	05/03/MUSTY	CL:2	Business-Marketing/Marketing-Fashion Merchandising/K.Moorman	
BL-BX	Religions	10/05/MUSTY Retain basic No propaganda	CL:1		
C	General auxiliary sciences of history	10/05/MUSTY Retain expensive	CL:1	General Studies/Social Studies/M.Carlson Health Services/ Hospitality Services ABE	
D	General history & Old world history	" "	CL:1		
E	General U.S. & American history	" "	CL:2		
F	U.S. Local history/Central & South America	" "	CL:2		
G	Geography/Anthropology/Recreation	" "	CL:2		
GN-GR	Anthropology/Folklore	15/05/MUSTY	CL:2	Business/Marketing Fashion Merchandising/K.Moorman	

MARIAN COURT JUNIOR COLLEGE
LINDSAY LIBRARY
COLLECTION DEVELOPMENT POLICY

PURPOSE

This document describes the policy by which materials are chosen for the Lindsay Library collection. This policy is guided by the mission statements of Marian Court Junior College and the Lindsay Library, and by the Library Bill of Rights (see Appendix A).

COLLECTING GOALS

Emphasis is placed on the educational and informational functions of the library within the college. The primary goal of all selection decisions is to support the curriculum of the college by fulfilling the needs of students for class-related research resources, material to supplement class work, and basic information sources. Fulfilling the immediate needs of instructors, administrators, and staff is an additional goal.

OBJECTIVE

Our primary objective is to obtain and provide access to high quality material at a level appropriate to the needs and abilities of two-year college students. This document defines the criteria by which selection decisions are made, and provides a detailed analysis by subject area of what level of collecting is desirable.

PRIORITIES

Priority is given to continuing support for the core curriculum: accounting and business; humanities, natural, and social sciences; microcomputers; secretarial sciences; travel, tourism and hospitality.

CRITERIA FOR CONSIDERATION

All library resources are selected with the general educational goals of the college in mind. The following criteria are considered in each decision to purchase. The work:

- is appropriate for use related to one or more courses in the curriculum or assignments regularly given.
- has educational significance; would contribute to the general education of a person.
- has literary merit, artistic quality, or social value.
- has been favorably reviewed by a reputable review source.
- has been recommended by a bibliography, professional journal, or member of the college community.
- has value due to timeliness, or due to longevity/permanence.
- has a high potential for use by members of the college community.
- is the product of a significant author, publisher, or producer.

- contributes to a balanced breadth of representation of a controversial issue; or provides an unbiased point of view.
- adds needed strength to a weak area of the collection; or helps to maintain an area of strength in the collection.
- is priced appropriately for the service/information it is expected to provide, or for the contribution it will make to the library collection.
- is appropriate for the reading level of the members of the college community who are expected to use it.
- is of good or superior technical quality (e.g. quality of paper, sound, or reproduction).

LIMITATIONS

All material collected is written or presented in the English language.

Textbooks are generally excluded.

Duplication of copies is avoided, except: when a duplicate of a frequently-used item is received as a gift; in cases where duplicate material in alternative formats makes long-term storage more feasible; or when a videotape performance of a work of drama or literature is acquired in addition to the text of that work.

Coffee-table books, vanity press books, and other works of non-substantive or ephemeral nature are generally excluded.

RESPONSIBILITY

The Corporation and the Board of Trustees of Marian Court Junior College are legally responsible for all matters relating to the operation of the college. Responsibility for selection of library material is delegated to the Director of Library Services, who works in cooperation with the members of the college community.

PROCEDURE

Day-to-day selection is done by the Director of Library Services. Support and guidance from members of the faculty and administration is obtained through meetings of the Library Committee (at least twice per year). Suggestions and specific recommendations are encouraged from all members of the Marian Court community, particularly the teaching faculty. Selection aids include professional review sources (Library Journal, Booklist, professional journals), bibliographies of appropriate subject areas, and individual recommendations. Retrospective collecting is based on sources such as Books for College Libraries and Books for Junior College Libraries, and on bibliographies for curricular subject areas (e.g. The Basic Business Library by Schlessinger). Needs that cannot be met at Marian Court's collecting level are referred to other libraries, particularly to members of the NECCUM cooperative. Collection evaluation and weeding are ongoing activities.

CHALLENGED MATERIALS

POLICY

Should an objection to a particular work in the Lindsay Library collection arise, members of the college community have the right to request that the selection be reconsidered. In the event of such a request, a hearing will take place as soon as possible after the request is received, and a timely response will be provided. The decision to retain or withdraw the challenged work will be made in light of the principles of intellectual freedom, as stated in the First Amendment to the Constitution of the United States and in the Library Bill of Rights (Appendix A). The work will remain available to library users during the time that the request for reconsideration is being heard.

PROCEDURE

- Complainant confers with the Director of Library Services, who will provide a Request for Reconsideration form to the complainant (see Appendix B).
- Complainant must fill out the form completely, including his/her name and address, and must unambiguously identify the work in question.
- An ad hoc committee consisting of the President, the Director of Library Services, at least one faculty member, and at least one student, will review the Request for Reconsideration as soon as possible after it is received. They will:
    - Read or view the challenged work in its entirety.
    - Refer to reviews and selection aids for professional opinions of the work.
    - Re-examine the selection decision in light of the selection criteria stated in this Collection Development Policy, and in light of the principles of intellectual freedom.
    - Present a written response to the complainant within a reasonable amount of time.

The ad hoc committee may choose to confer with the complainant in the process of making its decision.

GIFTS

Gift material will be judged in light of the selection criteria laid out in this document, and will be accepted or rejected for the collection on the basis of these criteria.

WITHDRAWALS

Collection development is an ongoing process that must include the removal of items that no longer fulfill the criteria laid out in this document. The decision to withdraw an item will be made in light of these criteria, taking into consideration the physical condition of the material as well as the educational value of the information. Worn, damaged, or lost items still of educational value will be replaced if possible.

DETAILED ANALYSIS FOR SUBJECT FIELDS

This analysis is arranged by Dewey classification (Abridged DDC, Edition 12), as is the Lindsay Library collection. The various collecting levels are defined in Guidelines for the Formulation of Collection Development Policies, David L. Perkins, editor (Collection Development Committee, Resources and Technical Services Division, American Library Association, 1979). The following descriptions are quotations from this document, and the collecting levels defined are used throughout Lindsay Library's Collection Development Policy.

Comprehensive Level

A collection in which a library endeavors, so far as is reasonably possible, to include all significant works of recorded knowledge (publications, manuscripts, other forms) for a necessarily defined field. This level of collecting intensity is that which maintains a "special collection"; the aim, if not the achievement, is exhaustiveness.
(Not used at Marian Court)

Research Level

A collection which includes the major published source materials required for dissertations and independent research, including materials containing research reporting, new findings, scientific results, and other information useful to researchers. It also includes all important reference works and a wide selection of journals and major indexing and abstracting reference services in the field.
(Not used at Marian Court)

Study Level

A collection which supports undergraduate or graduate course level work, or sustained independent study; that is, which is adequate to maintain knowledge of a subject required for limited or generalized purposes, of less than research intensity. It includes a wide range of basic monographs, complete collections of the works of important writers, a selection of representative journals, and the reference tools and fundamental bibliographical apparatus pertaining to the subject.
(Instead of this code, Marian Court uses the optional subcodes *Advanced Study Level* and *Initial Study Level*, which are defined below.)

Advanced Study Level

A collection which is adequate to support the course work of advanced undergraduate and master's degree programs, or sustained independent study; that is, which is adequate to maintain knowledge of a subject required for limited or generalized purposes, of less than research intensity. It includes a wide range of basic monographs both current and retrospective, complete collections of the works of more important writers, selections from the works of secondary writers, a selection of representative journals, and the reference tools and fundamental bibliographical apparatus pertaining to the subject.

Initial Study Level

A collection which is adequate to support undergraduate courses. It includes a judicious selection from currently published basic monographs (as are represented by Choice selections) supported by seminal retrospective monographs (as are represented by Books for College Libraries); a broad selection of works of more important writers; a selection of the major review journals; and current editions of the most significant reference tools and bibliographies pertaining to the subject.

Basic Level

A highly selective collection which serves to introduce and define the subject and to indicate the varieties of information available elsewhere. It includes major dictionaries and encyclopedias, selected editions of important works, historical surveys, important bibliographies, and a few major periodicals in the field.

Minimal Level

A subject area in which few selections are made beyond very basic works.

Out of Scope

The subject area is not collected.

300 Social Sciences

300 Sociology

300 Social sciences - standard subdivisions
301 Sociology & anthropology - interdisciplinary works
Basic level
Collect to support introductory electives in sociology, but not in anthropology.

302 Social interaction (including communication)
305 Social groups (including women and racial groups)
306 Culture & institutions (including marriage and family)
Initial study level
Collect to support sociology electives, including research topics. Maintain currency on social problems in the United States.

303 Social processes
304 Factors affecting social behavior
307 Communities
Out of scope

308 Not used
309 Not used

310 Statistics

Minimal level
Collect reference material only (e.g. almanacs). Collect current and historical statistics on the United States, and current and historical statistics on the state (Massachusetts only) and local area level. Collect only current material on foreign countries.

320 Political Science

Out of scope

330 Economics

330 Economics
331 Labor economics
332 Financial economics
333 Land economics (i.e. real estate)
337 International economics
339 Macroeconomics
Initial study level
Collect to provide theory and history, stressing the student's role in the system and how the theory relates to her future in the business world.

MODEL POLICY STATEMENTS

Partial Documents

McIntosh College Library
Dover, NH 03820

Collection Development Policy

Legal Studies Department
1993-94 Academic Year

Description of Collection

The non-circulating Law Library collection is designed to serve as the base for students in the paralegal and criminal justice programs of study. The holdings are listed in Attachment One.

The majority of the circulating collection contains print materials on the Constitution, its history and interpretations. Books on the history and organization of the American legal system, tax issues, criminal law, and business law are also included.

The circulating collection also focuses on print materials which support the criminal justice program specifically. These materials relate to criminal investigation, community policing, rape investigations, and domestic violence.

Courses supported by the collection are:

- Advanced Legal Skills
- Bankruptcy
- Business Law II
- Business Law I
- Constitutional Law
- Criminal Investigation
- Criminal Law
- Crisis Intervention
- Evidence
- Family Law
- Health Care Law
- Introduction to Security
- Introduction to Law Enforcement
- Introduction to Legal Studies
- Introduction to Criminal Justice
- Introduction to Security
- Landlord and Tenant
- Law Office Procedures
- Legal Research
- Police Procedures
- Police Procedures
- Probation, Parole and Rehabilitation
- Real Estate Law

The general reference collection includes the Landmark Decisions of the United States Suprem^ court series.

The National Institute of Justice library is available to students in vertical file format. A list of the topics is available in Attachment Two. The file is constantly being updated with new materials and articles. The reference section supporting the criminal justice program has information about career development as well as a few classics in the field.

Non-print materials include Crime File Series videos from the National Institute of Justice as well as others covering courtroom tactics and child sexual abuse. Other videos address the Constitution and legal careers.

Westlaw is an on-line collection of legal data bases. Federal and state statutes, as well as a variety of law reviews, are just a sample of what is available through Westlaw. Students have access to this service through a computer in the library.

Periodicals:

- FBI Law Enforcement Bulletin
- Federal Probation
- Law Enforcement News
- Legal Assistant Today
- National Law Journal
- National Institute of Justice Journal
- New Hampshire Bar News

Police
Police Chief
Problem Solving Quarterly
Subject to Debate
The Annotator
Trial Bar News

Description of Patrons

Students enrolled in the legal studies programs are divided between paralegal students and criminal justice students. They have various educational backgrounds. Many of these students have come directly from area high schools; others are re-entering the work force after many years or are changing career tracks. Some students in the criminal justice program are currently police officers who are completing requirements for an associate degree. Students enrolled in the one-year paralegal program come to the program with a college degree.

Selection Policy

Selection is done on recommendation of the chairperson of the Legal Studies Department and other members of the faculty. Publishers' materials, as well as standard core lists from the New Hampshire Bar Association and New Hampshire legal resource publishers, are also used a selection tools. Faculty requests continue to guide the selection process.

Retention and Weeding

Textbooks in the circulating collection are retained if they are not more than two years old. This assures that information is correct and updated. Workbooks and study guides are not longer collected. Only one copy of each item will be shelved. Textbooks used for class are on reserve and may be borrowed for one week only.

Development Plan

The Law Library collection will continue to be reinforced by the addition of treatises and restatements. Special attention will be given to those items which directly support new courses.

The circulating collection will continue to offer updated textbooks and books on topics of current interest. The classics in the field, as noted by the chairperson of the department, will be added to the collection.

Barbara Bolko, Librarian

of each item to the collection. Evaluation is also necessary to determine whether the College's aims, objectives, or goals have been achieved in building collections that are responsive to the needs of students, faculty, and staff.

G. Weeding Process

Weeding is the process of discarding or transferring to storage materials of all formats which are obsolete, unnecessary duplicates, rarely used, or worn-out. Regular weeding maintains the purposes and quality of library resources.

1. Legal Authority

Administrative Rule (6HX-10-3.018), Selection and Disposal of Learning Resources Materials, (Appendix M) and HCC Administrative Procedure (3.302), Disposal of Learning Resources Materials (Appendix J).

2. Responsibility

The Librarians have the main responsibility for weeding. Teaching faculty should be encouraged to provide input; however, the Librarians have final approval for the removal of any library/learning resources materials.

3. General Criteria To Weed/Remove Materials

a. Materials in poor condition. If heavily used, they should be replaced or repaired, if possible.

b. Duplicates no longer needed.

c. Older editions which have been replaced by newer ones.

d. Materials that have not circulated for three to five years and are not classics.

e. Materials that contain outdated or inaccurate factual content.

f. Materials which no longer support the curriculum.

g. Periodicals which are not indexed.

H. Challenged Materials

1. Legal Authority

HCC Administrative Procedure (3.510), Challenged Learning Resources Materials (Appendix N).

2. Procedure

On occasion, someone may question or challenge the suitability of certain materials found in the College collection.

A Library/LRC patron who approaches a staff member in person with such a challenge or question, will be referred to a Librarian.

Such questions will be met appropriately by the Librarian with reference to these collection development policy guidelines, including the Library Bill of Rights (Appendix B) and/or The Freedom to Read statement (Appendix C).

If a patron wishes to challenge formally the library's inclusion of an item, he/she will be directed to fill out the official "Request for Review" form and submit it to the Library/LRC.

Written challenges about any Library/LRC item, sent to any office in the College, will be referred to a Librarian on the campus where the item is housed.

A challenge of any item will be discussed by a Library Committee composed of the Library Cluster and the Associate Vice President of Learning Resources Services.

This Committee will respond to the challenger using the attached reply form.

In the interim, the challenged material will not be removed from its usual place in the collection.

3. Forms

a. Request For Review (see Appendix O)

b. Response To Review (See Appendix P)

APPENDIX J

ADMINISTRATIVE PROCEDURES

Title: DISPOSAL OF LEARNING RESOURCES MATERIALS	Identification: 3.302 Page: 1 of 4 Effective Date: January 12, 1993
Authority: SBE 6A-14.0262; 6A-14.0247 FS 240.319	Signature/Approval: [signature]

PURPOSE

The purpose of this administrative procedure is to establish procedural guidelines for disposing or removing library materials in a consistent manner.

PROCEDURE

To be current, useful and accessible, each campus library collection will be systematically evaluated on an ongoing basis to purge or remove materials in accordance with the following guidelines:

1. Materials may be disposed of due to appearance:
   - A. Books with antiquated appearance which may discourage use.
   - B. Books that are a part of badly bound volumes with soft pulpy paper and/or poorly bound.
   - C. Poorly printed books which includes works with small print, dull or faded print/illustrations, cramped margins or translucent paper with print showing through.
   - D. Old volumes with worn out, dirty, brittle and/or yellow pages, missing pages, frayed bindings, broken backs or dirty book coverings.
   - E. Audio visual materials which are worn, outdated or superseded.
2. Materials that may be disposed of due to lack of need:
   - A. Duplicated, unneeded copies.
   - B. Older, outdated editions.
   - C. Materials that do not meet the current selection criteria.

ADMINISTRATIVE PROCEDURES

Identification: 3.302	Page: 2 of 4	Effective Date: January 12, 1993

3. Materials that may disposed of due to content:
   - A. Materials that include dated information.
   - B. Materials that are poorly written.
   - C. Materials that include incorrect information.
   - D. Materials that have been replaced by improved editions.
   - E. Materials that include earlier titles in repetitious series.
4. The following specific classes of works may be disposed of in accordance with the following guidelines:
   - A. Ordinary Textbooks - when the work is over ten (10) years old.
   - B. Technology(ies) and Medicine (health care) - when the work is between five (5) and ten (10) years old.
   - C. Travel Books - when the book is over ten (10) years old, except when the work is a classic.
   - D. Economic, Business and Science Books - when the book is over ten (10) years old.
   - E. Fiction Best Sellers of Ephemeral Value - when the book is over ten (10) years old.
   - F. Social Science, Topical Material - when the book is over ten (10) years or fifteen (15) years old.
   - G. Encyclopedias - when new editions are purchased which is preferably every five (5) years. (The exception is for editions of recognized scholarly merit).
   - H. Almanacs, Yearbooks and Manuals - when the library receives the latest editions, the library will keep the older edition(s) for at least five (5) years. However, in excess of ten (10) years is the preferable time limitation based on individual merit.

I. Dictionaries - these books will be rarely disposed or removed from the library collections.

J. Directories - the library will generally only retain the current edition.

K. Inexpensive Geographic Sources - when the material is out of date between five (5) and ten (10) years. However, a library will rarely dispose of expensive geographic sources or those of historical value.

The Associate Vice President for Learning Resource Services will review the Records Management Reference Manual prior to disposal and contact the Records Management Officer where needed.

5. Periodicals and Serials may be disposed of in accordance with the following guidelines:

A. Periodicals that are not indexed may be removed.

B. Serials that are no longer published and without a cumulative index may be removed.

C. Early serial volumes, especially the longer serials (i.e., 50 or 60 volumes) may be removed.

D. Incomplete periodical or serial sets may be removed.

E. Specialized periodicals for courses and programs no longer offered may be removed.

F. Unused or inappropriate periodicals may be removed.

6. A campus Learning Resources Center will ensure that the appropriate records are deleted from the campus on-line circulation system for any removed library materials.

7. The campus Learning Resources Center will notify the Associate Vice President for Learning Resource Services of the removal. On a monthly basis, each campus Learning Resources Center will submit a report to the Associate Vice President for Learning Resource Services indicating the titles and dollar values of withdrawals of learning resources materials from the campus Learning Resources Center collections.

The Associate Vice President for Learning Resource Services' office will compile this information and generate a report to the Accounting Department on a quarterly basis. The Accounting Department will properly adjust the inventory value on the general ledger. Supporting documentation will be retained in the District Library Technical Services office.

8. The District Library Technical Services Department reports quarterly to the Accounting Department on all material withdrawn from the Learning Resources collection.

9. The Associate Vice President for Learning Resource Services his/her designee will delete the records from the district shelf list and from the Online Public Access Catalog (OPAC).

10. Prior to the disposal or removal of library materials, the appropriate library personnel will review the material. Library materials removed from a campus Learning Resources Center will be disposed of in the following priority:

A. dispensed to another campus library or group at the College;

B. offered to agreed-upon institutions or agencies within the area;

C. stored in the Warehouse for sale to students and/or the public; or

D. discarded at the discretion of the campus librarian.

11. Each campus Learning Resources Center will ensure that all library materials are reviewed on an ongoing and permanent basis.

Glendale College Library

WEEDING POLICY

To "weed" a collection means to examine titles carefully and remove materials which are dated, need mending or binding, or are worn-out. Materials which have low usage but which still have value as classics should be kept. Weeding serves to keep the collection attractive, pertinent, up-to-date and, therefore, more usable.

Philosophy

The Glendale College Library adopts the position that weeding is an integral part of collection maintenance and development. Systematic subject by subject evaluation of the existing collection and subsequent weeding of obsolete or seldom used materials supports the user's right of access to a broad spectrum of reading, listening, and viewing materials by providing an attractive and current collection.

Practice

The college library pursues a continuing program of collection analysis. In addition to acquiring new materials, it is important to remove from the existing collection those items no longer deemed useful because of the following factors:

inaccurate information
outdated information
lack of demand for material
physical condition
duplication of seldom used titles
superseded editions
newer material available on subject.

Recommendations for withdrawal of materials should be initiated by librarians with the advice of concerned faculty members when necessary. The input of other library staff members may also be requested.

The Reference Librarian is responsible for the development and maintenance of the periodical and reference book collections (including microforms). Exceptions are serials that are to be used by Technical Services, e.g., *Books in Print*, etc.

Guidelines for Discards

1. Books should be discarded if their physical condition includes

   a. Soiled pages (ink, grease, water marks, etc.)

   b. Yellowed, brittle paper

   c. Missing pages

   d. Missing illustrations, maps and charts

   e. Worn edges or corners of pages

   f. Broken spine that is wobbly and not mendable

   g. Dirty cover that is not washable

   h. Faded cover with illegible identification on spine which can not be relabelled

   i. Broken or separated hinges which can not be mended

2. Books which have an extremely poor usage record should be discarded.

3. Discard outdated books using subject area guidelines for collection maintenance.

4. Older editions of reference books may become circulating copies (after new editions are received) in cases where the works indicate by their date their relative value and/or a librarian or a faculty member has made a recommendation to that effect.

Subject Area Guidelines for Collection Maintenance

000

Titles in this area become dated rather quickly. Consider weeding after three to five years. For bibliographies, follow general subject guidelines.

100's and 200's

100's

100 - 129 PHILOSOPHY AND METAPHYSICS

Most materials in this area do not become dated. Update with current theories and schools of thought. Keep no more than 20 years, depending on the use of the materials.

130 - 139 POPULAR PSYCHOLOGY AND PARAPSYCHOLOGY

This area becomes dated as contemporary trends shift. Keep a title no more than five years if it is not used.

140 - 149 PHILOSOPHICAL VIEWPOINTS

Keep titles which provide a general overview of the field. Keep the standard authors (Comte, James, Mills) as a base; add current trends. Unused, "trendy" materials should be weeded within three to five years.

150 PSYCHOLOGY

Overview materials should be kept no more than ten years. Classic theories and psychoanalytic systems should be retained.

155 CHILD PSYCHOLOGY

Retain titles which are recognized as standard. Current theories generally become dated in five to ten years.

158 APPLIED PSYCHOLOGY

Some titles are very "trendy"; keep only three to five years as popularity and use dictate.

170 ETHICS

Changes in perspectives on theories (moral questions such as abortion, euthanasia) should be kept no longer than ten years.

180 CLASSIC PHILOSOPHY

Retain indefinitely representation from major classic schools.

200's

Retain most works in this area indefinitely. Consider weeding materials on new religious sects after five to ten years.

300's

Most books in this area deal with subjects of current interest and become dated in three to five years.

340's LAW

Currency is the key. Codes and regulations should be for the current year or latest edition.

350's POLITICS AND GOVERNMENT

Examine material five to fifteen years old for relevance.

371.425 CAREER BOOKS

Consider removal of books three years and older; (prospects in careers can change dramatically in that time). These books tend to include very specific information on salaries, job outlooks, certification requirements, etc.

EXAMINATION BOOKS

Content and focus do shift from time to time. For most college entrance exams anything older than five years is questionable. Civil Service Boards do make major changes in the content of examinations. Anything older than ten years should be examined carefully.

400's

Retain latest edition of standard works, dictionaries, rhyming dictionaries, lists of homonyms and antonyms, and some on verb conjugations. Stock grammars and dictionaries for languagues being offered in the curriculum. Keep <u>Webster's Modern New International Dictionary of the English Language</u>, second edition, indefinitely.

500's and 600's

For all subject areas not covered in the following recommendations, apply the general weeding guidelines, keeping in mind current usage and historical value. Topics such as mathematics, flowers, gardening, typing, welding, etc. should be kept until they are worn enough to be discarded since this type of material does not change rapidly. (The following are <u>general</u> guidelines and do not apply to every title in each category. Constraints of money and available replacement titles are often as important a consideration as the publication date.)

500's

Consider discarding after five years:

520 ASTRONOMY

523 STARS AND PLANETS

539 ATOMIC PHYSICS

575.1 GENETICS

576 MICROBIOLOGY

589.9 BACTERIOLOGY

Consider discarding after eight to ten years:

503 ENCYCLOPEDIAS/DICTIONARIES

537 ELECTRONICS

540 CHEMISTRY

574 BIOLOGY

590 ZOOLOGY

600's

Consider discarding after three to five years:

621.38 ELECTRONIC AND COMMUNICATION ENGINEERING

621.48 NUCLEAR ENERGY

629.13 AERONAUTICS

629.4 SPACE

Consider discarding after five to ten years:

621.47 SOLAR ENERGY

629.14353 SPACE/ROCKETS/MISSILES

641.1 NUTRITION

650 BUSINESS

658 MANAGEMENT

658.3 PERSONNEL MANAGEMENT

658.8 SALES

659.1 ADVERTISING

698 DECORATING

Consider discarding after ten years:

600 TECHNOLOGY

620 ENGINEERING

624 CIVIL ENGINEERING

630 AGRICULTURE AND RELATED TECHNOLOGY

610 - 619 MEDICINE AND RELATED FIELDS

In the medical fields it is necessary to exercise individual judgment to decide how much current value a title has and how much the basic information in it has changed as opposed to superficial or procedural changes. Here as in the field of law, currency is the key.

700's

Information in the 700's, particularly in the fine arts, does not become dated in the same manner as other areas of the collection. Weeding should be done cautiously, with careful attention to plates and illustrations.

703 & 709 ART DICTIONARIES, ENCYCLOPEDIAS, HISTORIES

Retain good single or multivolume encyclopedias with worldwide coverage published or updated within the last fifteen years. Retain basic works, especially the latest edition of art histories.

770's PHOTOGRAPHY

Check closely for outdated techniques and equipment.

780's MUSIC

Keep all basic materials, especially histories, unless they are worn and unattractive.

796's SPORTS

Maintain a basic collection with sports rules and regulations and how-to for major sports.

800's

The usual rules for discard do not apply to the 800's as the majority of the material does not become outdated. General works, 800-810, might be discarded after five years. Fiction titles tend to become outdated in the areas of ephemeral best sellers and mass market movie tie-ins. Peripheral fiction can be discarded when copies are worn. The rest of the 800's, as a rule, can be used indefinitely.

900's

Generally, titles in the 900's are useful for a longer period of time than are books in some other fields such as science, technology, and law. The main factors to consider are use, accuracy, facts and fairness of interpretation.

Reference titles should be scrutinized before discarding older editions. It should be determined whether or not a new edition supercedes an older one. Both books may need to be kept.

901 - 909 WORLD HISTORY AND CIVILIZATION

Retain standard works and documents.

910 - 919 GEOGRAPHY AND TRAVEL

Keep geographies as long as they are useful. Discard when newer edition is published or countries have had a change of name, boundary, or form of government.

Discard annual travel guides after five years. Weed personal narratives of travel over ten years old unless of high literary or historical value. Consider weeding general titles which have not been used in three years.

920 BIOGRAPHIES

Many books in this area can be kept indefinitely. Collective biography indexed in Biography Index should be retained.

930 ANCIENT HISTORY AND ARCHAEOLOGY

In general, retain. Consider weeding books which have not been used in five years.

940 - 999 HISTORIES OF SPECIFIC CONTINENTS, COUNTRIES, LOCALITIES

Discard personal narratives and war memoirs in favor of broader histories of World War II, the Korean War, and the war in Indochina unless the author is a local person or the book is cited in a bibliography as outstanding in style or insight. Discard stereotypical titles. Local history should be retained indefinitely. Retain books on the history and geography of the city; accounts of travels through the immediate area; biographies of local figures; local city directories. Keep most books by local authors (if of any literary value); and genealogies of important local families.

Lower Columbia College
Alan Thompson Library
1600 Maple Street
Longview, Washington 98632

GIFTS AND DONATIONS PROCEDURE

This is the procedure under which Lower Columbia College, Alan Thompson Library currently operates regarding donations of materials to the library:

> **Gifts are accepted with the provision that they will be evaluated for inclusion in the collection in the same manner as other materials, and unusable gifts will be sold, exchanged, or otherwise disposed of according to the discretion of the Associate Dean for Library Resources.**
>
> **The Library cannot legally appraise gifts for tax purposes. Donors are offered a signed and dated gift statement as a receipt.**

I have read and understand the above statement.

NAME:____________________________

DATE:____________________________

X. GIFT MATERIALS

A. The LRC welcomes gifts, but accepts them only with the understanding that it has the right to handle, dispose, house or provide access to the gifts in a manner which is in the best interest of the college, and that it retains unconditional ownership of the gifts accepted into the collection. Gift materials may be added provided they meet the library's criteria as previously expressed in the materials selection policy. Limitations of space, processing costs and physical condition are other considerations in the decision to accept gifts.

B. A commitment to accept gifts may be made only by the Technical Services Librarian. Donors are to be informed of the library's gift policy before materials are considered for acceptance.

C. An evaluation of materials is made by library staff before being accepted into the collection. If a gift is composed of more than 100 items, a library staff representative should visit the location where these items are housed. The staff member will select items considered most useful and these items will be further evaluated once received at the library.

D. Donors are requested to complete a gift materials form upon presentation of donated materials.

E. On request, the library will provide the donor with a list of items accepted. It cannot, however, assign a monetary valuation for tax or other purposes. On request, the donor will also be informed when materials are not accepted and will be asked to claim those unaccepted materials within one week of notification. After that time, the library will dispose of the materials as it sees fit and the items will not be considered to have been accepted by the library.

Guilford Technical Community College

M.W. BELL LIBRARY
GIFT MATERIALS

DONOR'S NAME:______________________________ DATE:__________

ADDRESS:______________________________

____

TELEPHONE NUMBER:______________________________

Thank you for donating these materials to Guilford Technical Community College's library collection.

Each title will be carefully examined to see if it will contribute to our collection development goals. After checking to see if we have this title or other edition, and whether or not we already have sufficient titles in the subject field, a final decision will be made as to which titles to accept or reject.

Please assist us in this process by answering in writing the questions listed below. Your generosity and cooperation are greatly appreciated.

1. Do you want us to notify you in writing as to how many titles we accept for the library's collection? (This letter is for income tax purposes; however, we do NOT place a cash value on donations.)

Yes__________
No__________

2. Do you wish to reclaim those titles that we do not accept into the collection?

Yes__________
No__________

3. Do you wish to have a gift plate added to each title you donated?

Yes__________
No__________

For further explanation of the library's gift policy, please see the Technical Services Librarian.

Staff member receiving (if Technical Services Librarian not available):______________________________

Action taken:______________________________

Rev. 10/90

St. Petersburg Community College

COLLECTION DEVELOPMENT POLICY
FOR PERSONS WITH DISABILITIES

(Approved by the Library Collection Development Committee, April 14, 1992)

OBJECTIVE:

To provide persons with disabilities equal access to information and sources under the provisions of the American with Disabilities Act (A.D.A.) and Section 504 of the Rehabilitation Act of 1973 to the extent possible within the mission guidelines of the M.M. Bennett Libraries.

PROCEDURE:

1. The Collection Development Librarian and/or others appointed by the Librarian-in-Charge at each site will read The Americans with Disabilities Act and Libraries: Questions and Answers, prepared by the Libraries Serving Special Populations Section of the Association of Specialized and Cooperative Library agencies, a division of American Library Association (on file in each site library) and other information about the A.D.A. and Section 504 of the Rehabilitation Act of 1973.

2. Each session ______________________________ will send a list of the disabilities currently represented by the student population at that site to the Librarian-in-Charge.

3. The Collection Development Librarian and/or others appointed by the Librarian-in-Charge at each site will conduct a self evaluation after notification by ____________________ to identify areas of the materials collection which need to be improved or made more accessible in order to meet the needs of the students and/or staff with disabilities. The self evaluation must:

    a. contain a list of the interested persons consulted;

    b. include students and/or staff with disabilities who use or are interested in the libraries to determine what kinds of formats your library should make available;

c. describe the areas examined and identify the problems;

d. describe the modifications made; such as borrowing special equipment from other sites or agencies, etc.

e. keep on file for three (3) years.

4. The Collection Development Librarian will develop resources as appropriate, and also will arrange to resource share with other libraries and agencies to meet the needs of the users with disabilities.

5. The Collection Development Librarian will make available to faculty and others involved in selection bibliographies available from the National Library Services for the Blind and Physically Handicapped (The Library of Congress, Washington, D.C. 20542) such as Reading Materials in Large Type, Reference Books in Special Media, Magazines in Special Media, Building a Library Collection on Blindness and Physical Disabilities; Basic Materials to use in selecting materials. Other bibliographies on disabilities can be acquired from:

a. National Captioning Institute
5203 Leesburg Pike
Falls Church, VA 22041

b. National Technical Institute for the Deaf
One Lamb Memorial Drive
P.O. Box 9887
Rochester, NY 14623-0887

c. Captioned Films/Videos for the Deaf
Modern Talking Picture Service
5000 Park Street North
St. Petersburg, FL 33709

d. Florida Department of State
Division of Library and Information Service
R.A. Gray Building
Tallahassee, FL 32399-0250

e. Florida Department of Education
Division of Blind Services
Bureau of Library Services for the
Blind and Physically Handicapped
420 Platt Street
Daytona Beach, FL 32114

f. National Rehabilitation Information Center
8455 Colesville Road, Suite 935
Silver Springs, MD 20910-3319

g. Another useful source for materials selection are special periodicals and newspapers dealing with disabilities. A list of some newsletters and periodicals have been given to the Collection Development Librarian at each site.

h. R.R. Bowker publishes The Complete Directory of Large Print Books and Serials which can be a selection tool.

6. The Collection Development Librarian at each site will make available resources for persons with disabilties, such as:

   a. Special materials dealing with disabilities, including resource directories

   b. Books in large type, braille, print/braille, audiotape, depending on the opinions of the users with vision impairments

   c. sign language books

   d. closed caption videos

   e. collection of special software programs for library users who are sight or hearing impaired to use with computers

f. CD Rom materials with the necessary equipment to scan standard print to turn it into an electronic format for enlargement, printing out in large print or Braille, and converting into speech.

g. computers with synthesized speech and large monitor displays and CD Rom players

h. a union list of specialized equipment available on each site

7. The emphasis in material selection for those persons with disabilities will be first, to provide materials to support college curricula; second, to provide materials on employment potential and possibilities for persons with disabilities; third, to provide materials creating awareness and attitudes toward acceptance of persons with disabilities. Sign language materials should be comprehensive and up to date.

TARRANT COUNTY JUNIOR COLLEGE DISTRICT

LEARNING RESOURCES

MATERIALS SELECTION POLICY

Introduction

Learning Resources is dedicated to the concept of a positive and innovative approach to the educational process, and to providing those materials and services most beneficial to the students, faculty, and staff. All materials acquired should reflect the resource needs and support the philosophy and mission of Tarrant County Junior College.

Tarrant County Junior College Mission Statement

Tarrant County Junior College is a comprehensive community college formed and brought into existence by its constituency to fill a need in the community for educational services. The College is committed to offering quality educational programs and services for the people of Tarrant County at a reasonable cost.

An open-door institution, the College provides a wide range of programs, including general academic, technical-vocational, student development services, continuing education, and community service. Through its board, administration, faculty, and staff, the College strives to ensure an environment conducive to learning.

Furthermore, the College emphasizes the educational development of its students and strives to encourage and promote excellence in instruction. The College is an institution committed to seeking and improving ways of facilitating the learning process.

The College recognizes and appreciates the diverse heritage of its constituency and strives to provide services and programs to meet the educational needs created by this diversity.

Accountable to the community it serves, The College is committed to responsible self-examination through which the quality of programs and services is continually assessed and evaluated.

Institutional Goals

The College has established specific goals that are modified as needed:

- To provide an administration and faculty that produce institutional effectiveness.
- To provide an open-door admission system that is responsive to the educational needs of its constituency and that reflects and upholds the standards of higher education.
- To provide appropriate academic courses that prepare students for completion of baccalaureate degrees.
- To provide technical-vocational instruction that prepares individuals for employment in the community.
- To provide developmental education that allows individuals to improve their basic skills.

- To provide continuing education and community services programs for individuals of varying ages and levels of education.
- To provide students with support services to help them meet their educational and personal goals.
- To provide and maintain buildings, facilities, and resources that enable individuals to achieve their educational goals.
- To encourage and support participation by students, faculty, administrators, and staff in activities, programs, and services that reflect the diverse cultural heritage of the College.
- To encourage professional development of all personnel through in-house and external programs and to recognize professional achievements.
- To provide ongoing assessment of programs, services, and personnel through planning, research, and evaluation.

Learning Resources Centers Mission Statement

The Learning Resources Program has the responsibility to provide:

A. An organized and readily accessible collection of materials and equipment needed to meet the institutional, instructional and individual needs of students and faculty;

B. Qualified and concerned staff committed to serving the needs of students, faculty, and community;

C. Leadership and assistance in the development of instructional systems which employ effective and efficient means of accomplishing educational objectives;

D. Facilities and resources which encourage innovation, learning, and community service; and

E. Other appropriate support in helping to perform the mission and meet the goals of Tarrant County Junior College.

Learning Resources Goals

In order to fulfill the responsibilities implied in the mission statement, the Learning Resources Program has the following goals:

1. To provide an organized collection of print and non-print materials which meets the identified needs of the college community.
2. To maintain the collection and related equipment in good physical condition.
3. To provide access to and control of Learning Resources materials through efficient distribution, circulation and reserve systems.

4. To enrich the college curriculum by working with faculty and staff in the design, development, and production of instructional programs and materials.

5. To enhance the quality of Learning Resources through participation in inter-library cooperation.

6. To provide bibliographic aids, point-of-use instruction, and personal assistance identifying, locating, and using information sources.

7. To provide an orientation and bibliographic instruction program designed to teach students how to use learning resources effectively.

8. To assist students and faculty in making effective and efficient use of learning resources.

9. To assist faculty and staff in locating and obtaining information through the use of local resources, data base searching and inter-library loan or purchase of materials.

10. To develop and maintain a capable Learning Resources staff through systematic programs of recruitment and career development.

11. To establish and maintain an effective liaison between the Learning Resources staff and the college community to assist in the planning, development, implementation, and systematic evaluation of programs and services that reflect the changing needs of the college.

12. To maintain accessible well-equipped facilities which encourage maximum use by the campus community.

13. To develop and administer policies and procedures which meet faculty and student needs and support the principles of intellectual freedom and individual rights.

14. To keep abreast of professional and technological developments with a view to applicability for Tarrant County Junior College.

15. To provide leadership and assistance in the use of educational technology and in the development of systems that support instructional objectives.

Statement on Intellectual Freedom

Tarrant County Junior College strongly supports the Library Bill of Rights (See Appendix A), the Freedom to Read statement (See Appendix B), and the Freedom to View statement (See Appendix C).

Statement on the Acceptance of Standards

Tarrant County Junior College operates under the rules and regulations of the Texas Higher Education Coordinating Board and the standards of the Commission on Colleges of the Southern Association of Colleges and Schools.

APPENDICES

CJCLS SURVEY OF COLLECTION DEVELOPMENT POLICIES

All figures are for fiscal year 92/93. If you supply figures from another time period, please indicate.

NAME AND TITLE ______________________________

LIBRARY/INSTITUTION ______________________________

____

PHONE ______________ FAX NUMBER ______________

INTERNET/BITNET ADDRESS ______________________________

Please place an "X" next to the appropriate response for each question.

1. Number of full-time equivalent (FTE) students, as listed in IPEDS report:

   __fewer than 1000
   __1000 - 3000
   __3000 - 5000
   __5000 - 7000
   __7000 - 10,000
   __more than 10,000

2. Number of full-time equivalent staff (include professional, paraprofessional, and clerical but do not include student assistants):

   __fewer than 5
   __5 - 10
   __10 - 15
   __15 - 25
   __25 - 40
   __more than 40

3. Size of collection; please list all statistics in terms of *titles*:

   a) total titles in your library's book collection

   __fewer than 25,000
   __25,000 - 50,000
   __50,000 - 75,000
   __75,000 - 125,000
   __125,000 - 200,000
   __more than 200,000

   b) total current periodical subscription titles; include both paid and free subscriptions:

   __fewer than 500
   __500 - 750
   __750 - 1000
   __1000 - 1500
   __1500 - 2000
   __more than 2000

   c) total number of audiovisual titles:

   __fewer than 1000
   __1000 - 2000
   __2000 - 3000
   __3000 - 5000
   __5000 - 7500
   __more than 7500

   d) total number of electronic titles; include CD-ROM, computer programs for public use, locally-mounted databases:

   __fewer than 20
   __20 - 30
   __30 - 50
   __50 - 100
   __100 - 200
   __more than 200

4. Size of your library's acquisition budget:

a) size of acquisitions budget for print materials; include books, pamphlets, documents, but not periodicals:

__less than $50,000
__$50,000 - $100,000
__$100,000 - $150,000
__$150,000 - $200,000
__$200,000 - $300,000
__more than $300,000

b) size of acquisitions budget for periodicals; include all subscriptions and microforms; do not include binding:

__less than $25,000
__$25,000 - $50,000
__$50,000 - $75,000
__$75,000 - $100,000
__$100,000 - $150,000
__more than $150,000

c) size of acquisitions budget for audiovisual materials; do not include equipment:

__less than $25,000
__$25,000 - $50,000
__$50,000 - $75,000
__$75,000 - $100,000
__$100,000 - $150,000
__more than $150,000

d) size of acquisitions budget for electronic resources; include online database searching, computer programs, CD-ROM titles, locally mounted databases, electronic journals, etc. Do not include your online public catalog.

__less than $5,000
__$5,000 - $15,000
__$15,000 - $30,000
__$30,000 - $50,000
__$50,000 - $100,000
__more than $100,000

e) total size of acquisition budget:

__less than $100,000
__$100,000 - $200,000
__$200,000 - $350,000
__$350,000 - $500,000
__$500,000 - $650,000
__more than $650,000

5. Does your library engage in any of the following alternatives to permanent ownership of materials? Check those that apply.

__ lease or rent audiovisual materials
__ purchase site or blanket licenses
__ videotape off-air or off-satellite
__ access resources for patrons through the Internet
__ participate in cooperative collection development with other libraries
__ perform online searches for patrons
__ offer interlibrary loan services
__ purchase documents on demand from commercial vendors; i.e. CARL, UMI, FirstSearch, etc.

6. For which, if any, of the following services does your library charge a fee?

FOR STUDENTS	FOR FACULTY	FOR COMMUNITY USERS	
			lease or rent audiovisual materials
			purchase site or blanket licenses
			videotape off-air or off-satellite
			access resources for patrons through the Internet
			participate in cooperative collection development with other libraries
			perform online searches for patrons
			offer interlibrary loan services
			purchase documents on demand from commercial vendors; i.e. CARL, UMI, FirstSearch, etc.

7. In using the above alternatives to ownership, what document delivery methods does your library use?
__U.S. mail
__telefax
__commercial delivery service; i.e. UPS, etc.
__Internet
__local or state-owned delivery service
__other, please explain:

8. What college departments assist the library in selection of materials of all types?
__academic departments
__instructional support services
__media centers
__academic computing departments
__other, please explain:

9. Do any of these groups share/assist with the library's selection of technology related to actual patron use of materials (such as CD-ROM drives, printers, etc.)?
__academic departments
__instructional support services
__media centers
__academic computing departments
__other, please explain:

10. Does your library have separate written collection development policies for the following? Check those that apply.

__print materials
__periodicals
__audiovisual materials
__electronic resources
__our library has one policy which covers all
__our library has no written collection development policies
__other, please explain:

11. Does your library have separate written weeding policies for the following? Check those that apply.

__print materials
__periodicals
__audiovisual materials
__electronic resources
__our library has one policy which covers all
__weeding is included in the collection development policies listed above
__our library has no written weeding policies
__other, please explain:

CJCLS PLANS TO PUBLISH A COLLECTION OF MODEL COLLECTION DEVELOPMENT AND WEEDING POLICIES. IF YOU ARE WILLING TO SHARE YOUR POLICIES LISTED ABOVE, PLEASE MAIL THEM BACK WITH THIS SURVEY.

Permission is granted to reproduce any or all of the attached policies, with proper attribution given to the contributing library. The copyright for the publication will be held by the American Library Association.

Your name	Title	Date

Please return this survey ***no later than August 15*** to:

Jennie S. Boyarski, Library Director
Paducah Community College
University of Kentucky
Alban Barkley Drive
P. O. Box 7380
Paducah, KY 42002-7380

We thank you very much for your cooperation!

TALLY OF SURVEY RESPONSES
CJCLS SURVEY OF COLLECTION DEVELOPMENT POLICIES

Please place an "X" next to the appropriate response for each question.

1. Number of full-time equivalent (FTE) students, as listed in IPEDS report:

35	0.17%	fewer than 1000	29	0.14%	5000 - 7000
62	0.31%	1000 - 3000	16	0.08%	7000 - 10,000
26	0.13%	3000 - 5000	24	0.12%	more than 10,000

2. Number of full-time equivalent staff (include professional, paraprofessional, and clerical but do not include student assistants):

47	0.23%	fewer than 5	26	0.13%	15 - 25
69	0.34%	5 - 10	14	0.07%	25 - 40
0	0.16%	10 - 15	13	0.06%	more than 40

3. Size of collection; please list all statistics in terms of titles:

a) total titles in your library's book collection

39	0.19%	fewer than 25,000	37	0.18%	75,000 - 125,000
73	0.36%	25,000 - 50,000	7	0.03%	125,000 - 200,000
46	0.23%	50,000 - 75,000	0	0.00%	more than 200,000

b) total current periodical subscription titles; include both paid and free subscriptions

132	0.65%	fewer than 500	8	0.04%	1000 - 1500
45	0.22%	500 - 750	0	0.00%	1500 - 2000
16	0.08%	750 - 1000	0	0.00%	more than 2000

c) total number of audiovisual titles

58	0.29%	fewer than 1000	28	0.14%	3000 - 5000
37	0.18%	1000 - 2000	22	0.11%	5000 - 7500
25	0.12%	2000 - 3000	21	0.10%	more than 7500

3. Size of collection; please list all statistics in terms of titles:

d) total number of electronic titles; include CD-ROM, computer programs for public use, locally-mounted databases

155	0.77%	fewer than 20	7	0.03%	50 - 100
16	0.08%	20 - 30	5	0.02%	100 - 200
9	0.04%	30 - 50	8	0.04%	more than 200

4. Size of your library's acquisition budget:

a) size of acquisitions budget for print materials; include books, pamphlets, documents, but not periodicals

120	0.59%	less than $50,000	7	0.03%	$150,000 - $200,000
57	0.28%	$50,000 - $100,000	2	0.01%	$200,000 - $300,000
16	0.08%	$100,000 - $150,000	0	0.00%	more than $300,000

b) size of acquisitions budget for periodicals; include all subscriptions and microforms; do not include binding;

109	0.54%	less than $25,000	4	0.02%	$75,000 - $100,000
62	0.31%	$25,000 - $50,000	6	0.03%	$100,000 - $150,000
19	0.09%	$50,000 - $75,000	2	0.01%	more than $150,000

c) size of acquisitions budget for audiovisual materials; do not include equipment

169	0.84%	less than $25,000	0	0.00%	$75,000 - $100,000
16	0.08%	$25,000 - $50,000	1	0.005%	$100,000 - $150,000
5	0.02%	$50,000 - $75,000	0	0.00%	more than $150,000

d) size of acquisitions budget for electronic resources; include online database searching, computer programs, CD-ROM titles, locally mounted databases, electronic journals, etc. Do not include your online public catalog.

90	0.45%	less than $5,000	8	0.04%	$30,000 - $50,000
65	0.32%	$5,000 - $15,000	2	0.01%	$50,000 - $100,000
27	0.13%	$15,000 - $30,000	0	0.00%	more than $100,000

4. Size of your library's acquisition budget:

e) total size of acquisition budget

122	0.60%	less than $100,000	4	0.02%	$350,000 - $500,000
52	0.26%	$100,000 - $200,000	0	0.00%	$500,000 - $650,000
19	0.09%	$200,000 - $350,000	1	0.005%	more than $650,000

5-6. Does your library engage in any of the following alternatives to permanent ownership of materials? Check those that apply?

		Alternative	Charge Students		Charge Faculty		Charge Community	
114	0.56%	lease or rent audiovisual materials	6	0.03%	15	0.07%	9	0.04%
88	0.44%	purchase site or blanket licenses	4	0.02%	9	0.04%	9	0.04%
128	0.63%	videotape off-air or off-satellite	2	0.01%	12	0.06%	9	0.07%
61	0.30%	access resources for patrons through the Internet	4	0.02%	6	0.03%	3	0.01%
71	0.35%	participate in cooperative collection development with other libraries	4	0.02%	3	0.01%	3	0.01%
138	0.68%	perform online searches for patrons	35	0.17%	36	0.18%	47	0.23%
198	0.98%	offer interlibrary loan services	33	0.16%	31	0.15%	26	0.15%
35	0.17%	purchase documents on demand from commercial vendors	12	0.06%	15	0.07%	9	0.04%

7. In using the above alternatives to ownership, what document delivery methods does your library use?

190	0.94%	U.S. mail	147	0.73%	telefax
105	0.52%	commercial delivery service	36	0.18%	Internet
93	0.46%	local or state-owned delivery service	8	0.04%	other (see attachment)

8. What college departments assist the library in selection of materials of all types?

197	0.98% academic departments	59	0.29% academic computing departments
82	0.41% instructional support services	19	0.09% other (see attachment)
52	0.26% media centers		

9. Do any of these groups share/assist with the library's selection of technology related to actual patron use of materials (such as CD-ROM drives, printers, etc.)

60	0.30% academic departments	108	0.53% academic computing departments
36	0.18% instructional support services	28	0.14% other (see attachment)
39	0.19% media centers		

10. Does your library have separate written collection development policies for the following?

35	0.17% print materials	131	0.65% our library has one policy which covers all
27	0.13% periodicals	27	0.13% our library has no written collection development policies
23	0.11% audiovisual materials	13	0.06% other (see attachment)
5	0.02% electronic resources		

11. Does your library have separate written weeding policies for the following?

16	0.08% print materials
6	0.03% periodicals
7	0.03% audiovisual materials
2	0.01% electronic resources
62	0.31% our library has one policy which covers all
69	0.34% weeding is included in the collection development policies listed above
43	0.21% our library has no written weeding policies
9	0.04% other (see attachment)

Total Surveys: 202

Contributing Institutions

Institution	Phone	Fax	Address
Austin Community College	512-495-7148	512-495-7200	P.O. Box 140526 Austin, TX 78714
Cedar Valley College	214-372-8140	214-372-8221	3030 N. Dallas Ave. Lancaster, TX 75134-3799
Chippewa Valley Technical College	715-833-6284	715-833-6470	620 W Clairemont Avenue Eau Claire, WI 54701-6162
College of the Desert	619-367-3591	619-367-3555	P.O. Box 139 Joshua Tree, CA 92252
College of DuPage	708-858-2800	708-858-8757	Lambert Road 33nd Street Glen Ellyn, IL 60137
Glendale Community College	818-240-1000	818-246-5107	1500 N. Verdugo Road Glendale, CA 91208-2894
Guilford Technical Community College	919-334-4822	919-841-4350	Mertys W. Bell Library P.O. Box 390 Jamestown, NC 27282-0309
Hillsborough Community College	813-253-7739	813-253-7794	P.O. Box 5096 Tampa, FL 33675-5096
Houston Community College System	713-630-1130	713-523-1438	1300 Holman Houston, TX 77004-3834
Lansing Community College	517-483-1657	517-372-7949	419 N. Capitol Avenue P.O. Box 40010 Lansing, MI 48901-7210
Lower Columbia College	206-577-2010	206-578-1400	1600 Maple Longview, WA 98632-0310
Marian Court Junior College	617-595-6768	617-595-3560	35 Little's Point Road Swampscott, MA 01907-2896
McIntosh College	603-742-1234	603-742-7292	23 Cataract Avenue Dover, NH 03820
Pierce College	206-964-6553	206-964-6713	9401 Farwest Drive SW Tacoms, WA 98498

Contributing Institutions

Institution	Phone	Fax	Address
St. Louis Community College	314-595-4484	314-595-4544	Florissant Valley Campus Library 3400 Pershall Road St. Louis, MO
St. Petersburg Junior College	813-341-3360	813-341-3368	P.O. Box 13489 St. Petersburg, FL 33733-3489
Tarrant County Junior College	817-656-6637	817-656-6601	North Campus 838 Harwood Road Hurst, TX 76054-3219
Warren County Community College	908-689-7614	908-689-9262	Route 57 West Washington, NJ 76054-3219
Washtenaw Community College	313-973-3379	313-677-2220	4800 E. Huron River Drive Ann Arbor, MI 48106

ABOUT THE EDITORS AND SECTION

Jennie S. Boyarski (MLS, Peabody College) is Library Director, Paducah Community College (PCC), University of Kentucky Community College System. Prior to joining PCC in 1967, she served as a middle school librarian. Boyarski recently authored a chapter, "Harnessing CD-ROMs and Collection Policies," *Community College Reference Services* and collaborated with Kate Hickey and others on an article on technostress for the periodical *Tech Trends*. Active in state and national library organizations, Boyarski serves on various committees and lectures on academic and public library issues.

Kate D. Hickey (MSLS, Clarion University) has been Director of the College Library, Pennsylvania College of Technology, since 1984. Previously she enjoyed an eclectic career as a reference librarian, a fisheries research librarian, and a children's librarian. Her recent professional activities include serving as chair of the Council of Pennsylvania Library Networks and being elected to the statewide Interlibrary Delivery Service Board.

The Community and Junior College Libraries Section, an active section of the Association of College and Research Libraries (ALA), has as its mission to contribute to library service and librarianship through activities that relate to libraries and learning resources centers that support the educational programs in community and junior colleges and equivalent institutions. This goal is implemented by more than a dozen standing and ad hoc committees reflecting the interests and activities of section members. The section supports awards, conference programs, and publishing ventures such as this volume.

INDEX TO THE DOCUMENTS